STAYING SAFE
IN AN UNSAFE WORLD

A GUIDE FOR COLLEGE WOMEN

BY ROBERT L. PARKE

Southern Yellow Pine
Publishing

Published by;
Southern Yellow Pine (SYP) Publishing
4351 Natural Bridge Rd.
Tallahassee, FL 32305

www.syppublishing.com

Cover Design by: Taylor Nelson

ISBN-10: 194086903X

ISBN-13: 978-1-940869-03-2

Printed in the United States of America
First Edition

ACKNOWLEDGEMENTS

To my granddaughter, a freshman at a Florida university, who, when I began talking with her about safety in college, said, "It won't happen to me!" You gave me the idea for this endeavor. I love you.

To the House Mother and President of "my" sorority at FSU, who agreed to let me talk to the Chapter members about safety for college women.

To the members of the Chapter who listened and demonstrated by their subsequent actions that they "got it."

To Mike Knowles, President and CEO of Seven Hills Security, Inc., who suggested that I "Write it up!"

To my beloved wife who has, as she always does, supported me throughout this project. Your patience has been remarkable. Your proofreading was invaluable. I love you.

Table of Contents

FOREWORD 1

INTRODUCTION 3

1

"BOOGEYMEN" AND MONSTERS 5

2

TED BUNDY'S MURDEROUS HISTORY 14

3

RAPE AND SEXUAL ASSAULT 25

4

ALCOHOL FACTS 39

5

"DATE RAPE" DRUGS 56

6

PERSONAL SAFETY FOR COLLEGE WOMEN 63

7

SELF DEFENSE TOOLS 92

FOREWORD

W. Ken Katsaris was the elected Sheriff of Leon County in Tallahassee, Florida from 1977-1981. That tumultuous time included the well-known terror spree of Ted Bundy. After reading and evaluating *Staying Safe in an Unsafe World* former Sheriff, W. Ken Katsaris, wrote the following comments endorsing this book.

Mr. Parke presents a thorough, well researched and thought-out compendium from his, and other professionals' experience. They represent a cross section of those involved in public safety, criminological research and psychological evaluations of the predator's mind, and the victim's vulnerabilities. With my experience directing the murder investigations that ultimately led to the capture, conviction, and execution of serial killer Ted Bundy for these crimes in Tallahassee, Florida, I can enthusiastically recommend Mr. Parke's book as a must read for all parents of children of any age, as well as police, medical, psychological, educational professionals -- and most especially female students who are embarking on a newly situated college or university life that brings new or different freedoms, eclectic friends, and associates. This new environment is particularly explored by Mr. Parke with information and safety protocols that have not heretofore been so candidly and thoroughly discussed.

Mr. Parke goes beyond discussion of the valuable safety compromises anyone can experience in any setting. Mr. Parke arms the readers with a plethora of easily implemented safety measures that enlighten. They then know how to navigate their environs with the confidence of knowledge, not fear.

W. Ken Katsaris

INTRODUCTION

The information in this book is a combination of my own experience as a police officer and investigator, along with the results of much research into safety issues, facts and statistics. Sources varied somewhat in the statistics they presented, but all were reasonably within the range of those cited here. At the end of each chapter, there will be a list of resources if additional information is needed.

Sadly, the world we live in is very unsafe. The more oblivious we are to our surroundings, the more we deny that "it" could happen to us, the more likely we are to be victimized. This book is not a clove of garlic to keep away vampires. It is not a suit of armor to foil any possible attempt to hurt you. It contains warnings and practical solutions.

It will not keep you from all potential harm. Planes and trains crash, hurricanes flood and tornadoes destroy. Mass killers, as opposed to serial killers, may strike anywhere, at any time, as they did at Sandy Hook Elementary School in Newtown, Connecticut and at the movie theater in Aurora, Colorado. There is little we, as individuals, can do to stop such things from happening other than trying to be as alert as possible. Nevertheless, when it comes to our own personal safety, there is a great deal we can do.

I have attempted to cover as much information as can reasonably fit into a relatively short and easy-to-read book. The goal is to help you learn the dangers, how to avoid them, and then to practice what you have learned. You will be safer. Your college experience will be better for it.

In my days as a police officer, and still, a shift begins with attendance at a meeting we called "Read-off" prior to hitting the street. This is when officers going on duty receive information from the shift Sergeant about wanted persons, stolen vehicles, crime patterns, and all the other things they need to watch for during their tour of duty. The very good and true-to-life 1980's TV show, "Hill Street Blues," began each episode with "Read-off." At its close, the shift Sergeant always said these words, which I share with you:

"Be careful out there!"

Robert L. Parke

Readers should be aware that Internet Web sites offered as citations and/or sources for further information may have changed or disappeared between the time this was written and when it is read.

1

"BOOGEYMEN" AND MONSTERS

When we were small children, sometimes our well-meaning parents, aunts, uncles and grandparents would warn us about the "Boogeyman." When we got older, we learned there was no such thing. The "Boogeyman" is a fictional being that exists, in one form and name or another, in many cultures around the world and is used to intimidate children into eating their dinner, going to sleep, coming in when called, or behaving. The warning is that the "Boogeyman" will "get you if you don't!" The name may have derived from "Buggy Man," the driver of the cart picking up corpses during the Black Plague of Europe. Unfortunately, in today's world, "Boogeymen" are real—and they are monsters.

What is a monster? It is anything that may come at you with the intent of doing you great harm or killing you. A Great White Shark is a monster if you are in the water and it suddenly grabs you. It is not personal to the shark. He's hungry and thinks you are a seal. He doesn't care if you are a child, a young woman or an old man. It can be cancer, which will do its best to kill you. The shark can be avoided by staying out of its water. Cancer can many times be defeated by fighting back. It is personal with cancer, but not consciously so. Two-legged monsters attack to make a statement or for personal gratification. They walk among us—and have for centuries. This book is about avoiding them and fighting back.

Oxford Dictionary gives this definition of (the two-legged) Monster: "An inhumanly cruel or wicked person." There are other definitions, all very similar, and it is this monster with which we should be concerned. This one wants to make you a victim for one of many reasons. It may be a political statement as in the case of the September 11 hijackers who flew airliners into the World Trade

Center towers, the Pentagon and a field in Pennsylvania, killing nearly 3,000. The two brothers who detonated two bombs at the finish line of the Boston Marathon, killing three and injuring many others, were making a political statement. There is not much we, as individuals, can do to thwart the political terrorist monster. We have no choice but to rely upon our police and security agencies, but that does not mean we should not remain vigilant and report anything our common sense and instinct tells us is, or could be, wrong. Bombings have been prevented by citizens who noticed a suspicious package and reported it to the police.

The human predator monster may be someone who focuses his rage on a particular group of people, or derives sexual gratification from killing. This monster may kill once, or many times. He may just rape, or he may rape and kill his victims. He may be a dedicated serial killer and/or rapist. He may also be the ordinary college guy who, under the influence of alcohol and raging testosterone, becomes a temporary monster who victimizes a coed unable to resist because of his overpowering strength or her being intoxicated or drugged. An encounter with any of these is a life-ending, or at least life-changing, event.

Serial killer monsters have been around for centuries. Jack the Ripper terrorized London for just over one month in 1888, killing and butchering at least five women, and was never caught.

Out of the, at least, 200 identified American serial killers, here are a few of the more infamous:

Albert DeSalvo, the "Boston Strangler," confessed to murdering 13 women in Boston between 1962 and 1964, most of whom were elderly and alone. He had a long history of committing petty crimes, and was discharged by the Army for disobeying orders. Years later, he settled down, married and had two children, one of whom was handicapped. He was considered to be a good family man and was well-liked by his colleagues and his employer.

David Berkowitz, "Son of Sam," killed seven people at random in New York City in 1976-1977. He had been born out of wedlock, and his mother gave him up for adoption. That apparently caused him to develop an inferiority complex toward women. In 1974, according to Berkowitz, he "heard voices" in his head telling him to kill, and he began randomly shooting couples in their cars. He worked as a postman.

Jeffrey Dahmer was the Milwaukee, Wisconsin serial killer who targeted young boys and men, killing 17. He kept body parts and skulls of his victims in his apartment for sexual gratification. He picked up his victims in gay bars, then drugged them, and killed them by strangulation. He served in the Army, but was kicked out after two years for drunkenness. He worked in a chocolate factory.

John Wayne Gacy, the "Killer Clown," murdered at least 33 men and boys, and buried some of them under the floor of his Chicago home. Gacy was a good businessman who developed a contracting company. He threw street parties for his friends and neighbors. He dressed as a clown to entertain children at local hospitals and was quite active in civic organizations. His friends and acquaintances saw him as a generous, friendly, hardworking member of the community.

Henry Lee Lucas was born to abusive alcoholic parents and his mother was a prostitute. He murdered his mother in 1960 and served time in prison until he was paroled. He subsequently attempted to kidnap a fifteen year old girl at gunpoint, and was again imprisoned. He was paroled in 1975, killed at least two more women, and was arrested yet again in 1983. He eventually confessed to hundreds of murders.

Dennis Rader, the "BTK" killer (Bind, Torture, Kill), murdered ten people in Kansas. The first four, in 1974, were a husband, wife and their two children in their home. As a child, Rader was apparently normal and unremarkable. He was a Boy Scout and participated in church youth group activities. He later admitted to having childhood fantasies of bondage, control and torture while he was still in elementary school. He also admitted to killing dogs and cats by hanging them. Later, Rader joined the Air Force where his service was acceptable and unremarkable. After his discharge, he married and held several jobs. He and his wife had a child, and Rader became active in his church and was a Boy Scout leader. All the while, he continued his murdering. He was not identified and captured until 1985. He received a sentence of 175 years.

Gary Ridgway, "The Green River Killer," murdered by strangling at least 48 young women in the state of Washington. He was raised in the state of Washington, and had a "troubled" childhood with parents who violently fought and a mother who was domineering. He joined the navy and saw combat in Vietnam. He married his childhood sweetheart and then two others. All ended in divorce. Like Ted Bundy, Ridgeway often returned to have sex with the bodies of the women he had murdered. He was eventually caught and was sentenced to 48 consecutive life terms.

Danny Rolling killed five students, four women and one man, in the space of one week in Gainesville, Florida, home of the University of Florida. He decapitated one and left her head in a bookcase. He, too, had a terrible childhood, suffering abuse, beatings and bullying by his father without support from his mother who refused to protect him. Rolling had been married and had a daughter. He enlisted in the Air Force, but was discharged after only two years because of drug and alcohol problems. He spent years burglarizing and robbing, which continued until he was arrested for the Gainesville murders on September 11, 1990. At that time, he was linked to murders in Shreveport, Louisiana in 1989.

Anthony Sowell, a/k/a "The Cleveland Strangler," raped and murdered 11 women between 2007 and 2009. He had recently been released after serving 15 years in prison for sex crimes. His life was, except for his earlier sex crimes, rather unremarkable. During the time of his Cleveland murders, he was noted as having a terrible stench about his person—no doubt from being around the decomposing bodies kept at his home. One shopkeeper said he had to open his front and back doors to air out his store after a visit from Sowell.

Charles Manson formed his own little cult he called "The Family" and ordered them to kill everyone at a Los Angeles home. On August 9, 1969, four of Manson's "Family" murdered actress Sharon Tate (wife of Roman Polanski, the movie director), her unborn daughter, and four other people who were visiting at the house. The next night, Manson's followers killed a husband and wife in their home. As a sad commentary on some parts of our society, Manson, who has been in prison for more than 42 years, has received more mail than any other prisoner in US history.

Psychiatrists, psychologists, sociologists and law enforcement have studied the phenomenon of the serial killer for decades. One area of examination is the childhood of the killer. That seems difficult to pin down as a sole causation. Serial killer Henry Lee Lucas had a childhood that was beyond horrific. One could reasonably conclude that there was no way he could have survived that and become anything less than a monster. On the other hand, Dennis Rader, the "BTK" killer, had an apparently normal childhood. He joined the Air Force where he served for four years and stayed in the Reserves for two more years. He married and attended college. He was gainfully employed. After his capture, he admitted that he had childhood fantasies about what it would feel like to strangle someone. The formative years of these two serial killers couldn't have been more different, although, most serial murderers seem to have had childhoods that were at least unusual in one way or another.

Some predator monsters do not kill their victims, and not all abduct college-age women. Sometimes they prey on younger children. Some of Ted Bundy's victims were as young as twelve. The predators may abduct and imprison them, sometimes for years, subjecting them to serial rape and sometimes killing them.

At age 14, Elizabeth Smart was kidnapped in Utah by a man and his wife. She was held—and raped—for nine months. Here's how she (partially) described her experience:

> "I felt like I'd been broken. I felt like my soul had been shattered. I just remember lying there, crying, being in so much pain physically and emotionally that I ended up falling asleep, and the last thought was of those children I had seen in the news. I remember thinking, they're lucky. I wish I was one of those children, because no one will ever be able to hurt them again." The experience showed her "what can happen, and how nobody is immune from pain, from suffering. No one can say, well, that's not going to happen to me, or my daughter or my son. It can. It's a very real danger." In her own house, her family has gone from "check and double check" to "triple and quadruple check."

Jaycee Dugard was taken in Lake Tahoe, NV, when she was eleven, and was imprisoned for 18 years by Phillip Garrido and his wife, Nancy. Garrido was a convicted sex offender. At the time he kidnapped Jaycee, he had recently been released on parole after serving only ten years of a 50 year sentence.

Most recently, three young women were rescued from the home of Ariel Castro in Cleveland, Ohio where they had been held since the years 2002 to 2004 from the ages of 14, 16 and 20. They were all physically, sexually and emotionally assaulted for the entire time they were in captivity. One became pregnant, and Castro repeatedly starved and beat her to cause several miscarriages. At his sentencing, Castro said, "These people are trying to paint me as a monster. I'm not a monster. I'm sick." Castro hanged himself with a bed sheet in his prison cell on September 3, 2013. He obviously could not face what he had dished out to his three victims for years.

Sure, Castro was sick, but no less a monster. It can be argued that every serial rapist or serial killer is "sick." They are called sociopaths and psychopaths, but unless you choose to study the behavioral sciences, the pathology of monsters is not your concern, however avoiding them is.

The abductors of Elizabeth Smart, Jaycee Dugard and the three young Cleveland women made sex slaves of their victims. They did so for personal gratification. Many more children—both girls and boys—become sex slave victims for monetary profit to human traffickers who can be thought of as monsters on steroids. If you are driving down the street, usually in a seedy part of town, and see one or more girls or young women standing around, provocatively dressed, and apparently soliciting male passersby, the odds are great that they started as unwilling participants in prostitution.

There are hundreds of thousands of sex slaves in the United States. Many started as runaways, others were abducted by for-profit human traffickers. The FBI reports that human sex trafficking is "big business. It is the fastest-growing business of organized crime and the third-largest criminal enterprise in the world." Children in foster care seem to be the most vulnerable for being sold into prostitution.

Any child who has a history of drug abuse or running away is at high risk for being abducted, threatened, beaten, raped and then sold into sex slavery. Young women or boys who are scooped up off the street by an abductor in a vehicle are at risk of being raped and forced into prostitution. Once they are repeatedly drugged to the point of addiction, threatened and even beaten, they become so emotionally and psychologically traumatized that they will not even try to escape. The average age of the girls is twelve, and the boys' average age is thirteen. Women are much more at risk of sexual assault or rape than men, but men are equally at risk of robbery and alcohol-related misfortunes, including injury and death.

Law enforcement officials in Ohio report that the three most common methodologies used by traffickers to recruit their victims are drugs, the internet and elements of force, fraud or coercion, including abduction.

Ted Bundy was perhaps the most notorious of all serial killers. The following chapter is about him. As Bundy focused entirely on young women, many of them college women, it is particularly instructive to examine how he did what he did. His methodology took advantage of the failures of young women to pay attention to their surroundings, to allow themselves to become isolated, and to be entirely too trusting. Bundy is most remembered for the Chi Omega sorority house murders at Florida State University, but most of his crimes were perpetrated on women who were just "out and about" the business of their lives.

Bundy has had plenty of company. A study by Radford University indicates over 2,000 serial killers have been active in the United States from 1900 through 2010. Of these, nearly 1,700 have been active since 1970. Their numbers seem to grow.

It seems likely that rapists and serial killers will be around for a very long time, if not forever. Law Enforcement does everything it can, but is almost always called in after the fact. The most effective guard against these monsters is you. This chapter acquaints you with the monsters. This book can teach you behavior patterns that will increase your ability to avoid the monsters and stay safe in this very unsafe world.

This is not fiction. It's very real, and it can save your lives. Please take it seriously. The following chapters will demonstrate the vulnerabilities of young people who don't understand that this world is unsafe. It will serve as a beginning to their education about staying safe in an unsafe world.

References

Frater, J. (n.d.). Retrieved from http://listverse.com/2009/10/24/15-bogeymen-from-around-the-world/

Jack the Ripper. (2013). *The Biography Channel website*. Retrieved from http://www.biography.com/people/jack-the-ripper-9351486.

Albert DeSalvo. (2013). *The Biography Channel website*. Retrieved from http://www.biography.com/people/albert-de-salvo-17169632.

IMDb. (2011). Retrieved from http://www.imdb.com/name/nm0075473/bio

Montaldo, C. (2010). Retrieved from http://crime.about.com/od/serial/a/dahmer.htm

Bell, R. (2011). *Turner Entertainment*. Retrieved from http://www.trutv.com/library/crime/serial_killers/notorious/gacy/gacy_1.html

Henry Lee Lucas. (2013). *The Biography Channel website*. Retrieved 10:02, Oct 20, 2013, from http://www.biography.com/people/henry-lee-lucas-11735804.

Jamal, J. Dennis rader- btk killer [Web log message]. Retrieved from http://dennisraderbtk.blogspot.com/

Blanco, J. (n.d.). Retrieved from http://murderpedia.org/male.R/r/ridgway-gary.htm

Steel, F. (2011). Retrieved from http://www.trutv.com/library/crime/serial_killers/predators/rolling/gain_1.html

Kennedy, H. (2009). *Daily News website*. Retrieved from http://www.nydailynews.com/news/national/ohio-rapist-anthony-sowell-lived-rotting-bodies-women-strangled-cleveland-police-article-1.413334

Rosenberg, J. (n.d.). Retrieved from http://history1900s.about.com/od/1960s/p/charlesmanson.htm

Henry Lee Lucas. (2013). *The Biography Channel website*. Retrieved 10:02, Oct 20, 2013, from http://www.biography.com/people/henry-lee-lucas-11735804.

Ritz, E. (2013). *Kidnapping victim elizabeth smart shares the best advice she's ever received with theblaze*. Retrieved from http://www.theblaze.com/stories/2013/07/05/kidnapping-victim-elizabeth-smart-shares-the-best-advice-shes-ever-received-with-theblaze/

Hawkins, K. (2012). *The Backyard Prisoner: The Story of Jaycee Dugard.* Retrieved from http://www.trutv.com/library/crime/criminal_mind/sexual_assault/jaycee_dugard/1.html

McLaughlin, E., & Brown, P. (2013). *Judge sentences cleveland kidnapper ariel castro to life, plus 1,000 years.* Retrieved from http://www.cnn.com/2013/08/01/justice/ohio-castro

Aamodt, M. G. A. (n.d.). Retrieved from http://maamodt.asp.radford.edu/Serial Killer Information Center/Serial Killer Statistics.pdf

Carroll, S. (2013, October 3). As state battles child sex trafficking, more resources needed. *HeraldTribune.com.* Retrieved December 9, 2013, from http://www.heraldtribune.com/article/20131003/ARTICLE/131009834

Craig, C. (2013, October 23). Protect foster children from sex trafficking: Column. *USA Today.* Retrieved December 8, 2013, from http://www.usatoday.com/story/opinion/2013/10/23/children-sex-trade-foster-care-column/3153537/

Swift, J. (2013, October 4). Top Researchers Say More Must Be Done to Address Child Sex Trafficking in United States. *Juvenile Justice Information Exchange.* Retrieved December 9, 2013, from http://jjie.org/top-researchers-say-more-must-be-done-to-address-child-sex-trafficking-in-united-states/

Smith, A. (2013, October 23). Sex slavery: what can students do about it? *The Independent Collegian.* Retrieved December 9, 2013, from http://www.independentcollegian.com/news/sex-slavery-what-can-students-do-about-it-1.2842713#.UnLyDvlOOSo

2

TED BUNDY'S MURDEROUS HISTORY

No discussion of safety for young women would be complete without examining the murderous career of Ted Bundy. His abductions and attacks were successful, in part, because of his good looks and charismatic charm, but mainly he succeeded because of personal, residential, and situational security lapses by his victims. Bundy did not limit his attacks to women on college campuses. Many of his assaults were directed toward college women and all were against young women and girls. Some of this history may be painful to read, but by doing so, you will gain additional insight into the particular hazards young women may encounter—before, in, and after college. As you read, try to identify the things that helped Bundy get access to his victims.

Theodore Robert Bundy was born in 1946 to an unmarried mother. In those days, that was almost always socially unacceptable. To hide the fact that Ted was illegitimate, his mother, Eleanor, moved to the home of her parents in Philadelphia, and raised him as the adopted son of his grandparents. Bundy was told that his mother was his sister. A few years later, she and Ted moved to Tacoma, Washington, and she married Johnnie Bundy, with whom she had several more children. The Bundys appeared to be a content, working-class family.

Even as a young child, Ted had begun demonstrating unusual behavior. He developed a fascination for knives and, as a teenager, started peeking in windows. He became a thief and a suspected burglar.

Bundy's murdering of young women may have begun as early as the late 1960s in California. Robert Keppel, the Seattle police detective who interviewed Bundy in Florida, said that Bundy attended Stanford University near Santa Rosa in 1968. He also had a girlfriend he would visit in Palo Alto, California. During these interviews, Bundy referred vaguely to murders he had committed in California. Keppel stated,

> "Bundy is definitely a good suspect. The killings in Santa Rosa would fit his methods, he spent time in the area, and I'm sure he started killing well before 1974. One of the last times I talked to Bundy, I mentioned California, and he looked at me like, 'I can't talk about that right now'. I think he believed his execution would be stayed so he could talk for years about his crimes, but the governor had other ideas."

Keppel believes Bundy was responsible for the murders of seven young women around Santa Rosa, California. An eighth victim disappeared and has never been found. These are known as the Santa Rosa Hitchhiker Murders.

During his time at the University of Washington, Bundy gave the appearance of being a completely normal person. He impressed his professors and fellow students with his intelligence and personality. He was outwardly confident and was described as charming and charismatic. He was politically and socially active. While at the university, he fell in love with a dark-haired young woman who was wealthy and pretty, and who was from an influential family. When they broke up, Bundy was devastated. Many of his later victims had a passing resemblance to her.

He graduated from the University of Washington in 1972 with a degree in Psychology, and was accepted into law school in Utah. Around that time, women in the Seattle area and in Oregon began disappearing. Some authorities believe that Bundy began his killing rampage around the end of 1973 or in early 1974, but Detective Keppel, as quoted above, believes it was earlier than that. There was talk about some of the victims last being seen in the company of a young dark-haired man called "Ted."

Bundy often lured his victims into his car by pretending to be injured and asking for their help. Their kindness proved to be a fatal mistake. Playing on sympathy, Bundy wore his arm in a sling, and a fake cast on his leg. He would ask his victims to help him carry or load things into his car. Once the victims got in his car or were leaning into his car, he would hit them in the head with a crowbar or pipe. After striking his victims, he would handcuff them to immobilize them and then kill them.

Bundy sometimes raped his victims, if they were still alive, before beating or strangling them to death. Frequently, he killed them first and then had sex with their corpses. Sometimes he would even return to them until decomposition made it unbearable. Psychologists have analyzed Bundy's personality and behavior, and diagnosed him as having "Schizoid necrophilia."

In 1975, after Bundy moved to Utah to attend law school, he was stopped by police and they found what they considered to be burglary tools in his car—a crowbar, a face mask, rope and handcuffs. He was arrested for possession of these tools and the police began to suspect him of much more serious crimes.

He was arrested again in 1975 for the kidnapping of a young Utah woman, Carol DaRonch, who escaped and survived. She was approached at a Salt Lake City shopping mall by a man who identified himself as an undercover police officer. He told her that her car had been broken into and that she needed to go with him to the police department to make a report. After getting in his car, she noticed alcohol on his breath and that they were actually headed away from the police department. She refused to buckle her seat belt. Bundy stopped the car and managed to put a handcuff on one of her wrists but not the other. Threatened with a gun and a crowbar, she fought him off and rolled out of the car. She then flagged down another motorist as Bundy drove away.

Later that same day, another young woman disappeared after leaving a high school event in nearby Bountiful, Utah. A handcuff key was found in the school parking lot. She was never seen again.

Bundy was convicted of the DaRonch kidnapping, and received a one to fifteen-year prison sentence.

Two years later, Bundy was indicted on murder charges for the death of a young Colorado woman and was extradited from Utah to Colorado. In that case, he decided to act as his own lawyer and was given law research privileges. While at the courthouse library, he jumped out of a second story window and escaped. He was captured eight days later.

After being rearrested, Bundy again escaped from custody. In December, 1977, after dieting to lose weight, he squeezed through a hole he had made in the ceiling of his cell, and crawled through the area above the ceiling to a Deputy's room where he changed clothes. He then simply walked out of the building. Authorities did not discover that Bundy was missing for over 15 hours, giving him an insurmountable head start on the police.

This time, Bundy was not so quickly recaptured. He made his way to Tallahassee, Florida by way of an airline flight to Chicago, a stolen car to Atlanta, and a bus to Tallahassee. He rented an apartment, under a fictitious name, near Florida State University, getting along on stolen credit cards, shoplifting and stealing purses.

There, in the early morning hours of January 14, 1978, after being seen in the tavern next door, Bundy entered the Chi Omega Sorority house at FSU by way of an exterior door that was not secured. He attacked four of the young women residents with a length of tree branch he had picked up outside. Two of them were killed and the surviving two were grievously injured. The deceased sisters were bludgeoned and then strangled with panty hose. The survivors were bludgeoned, but not strangled.

The two injured women may have survived only because another sister came home during the attacks, possibly alerting Bundy. As she entered, she noticed the door to the house was ajar. She heard footsteps above her coming down the stairs from the second floor and quickly hid. She saw the profile of a man wearing a blue cap and carrying a "log" leave the house by way of the front door. She then went upstairs to awaken her roommate. They returned downstairs to check the front door, then again went upstairs to awaken the chapter president. While the three were talking in the hallway, a badly injured sister opened her door and began staggering away from the others. They started after her to check her condition, and, as they passed her open door, saw her roommate sitting on the edge of her bed, bleeding profusely from severe facial injuries.

When the police arrived, they found the dead and injured sisters. One of the deceased sisters had been violently bitten by Bundy. The bite marks were later compared to Bundy's teeth and were a match.

There are significant disparities about how Bundy gained entry to the sorority house. The Sheriff of Leon County, Florida at the time of the Chi Omega murders was W. Ken Katsaris. To resolve the question, Mr. Katsaris was contacted. He is presently a nationally known expert consultant in the areas of law enforcement agency policies, practices and customs, campus rapes and assaults, failure to protect specific persons, and inadequate premises security. Mr. Katsaris advised that the Leon County Sheriff's Office investigation, along with that of the Tallahassee Police Department, revealed that Bundy entered through an exterior door that was either vulnerable to a credit card pushing aside the latch bolt or, more likely, a door that had been propped open. Mr. Katsaris stated that the latter scenario was found by investigation to be not uncommon.

Bundy left the sorority and went to a two-apartment residence a few blocks away. He entered one of the apartments, apparently through a window, and attacked Cheryl Thomas in her bed. At about 4 AM, the victim's neighbors heard loud banging noises, and the sound of her moaning. They did not immediately realize what was happening. They called Ms. Thomas, and after receiving no answer, one yelled, "Call the police." The police found what they believed to be a mask made from panty hose with eye-holes cut out. Cheryl Thomas survived, but the attack severed one of her auditory nerves, leaving her completely and permanently deaf in one ear. She suffered other grievous injuries, including five skull fractures, a broken jaw, and a dislocated shoulder. She was hospitalized for a lengthy period of time.

By February 6, 1978, Bundy had stolen a white van from the FSU Media Center, changed its license plate and traveled to Jacksonville, Florida, where he unsuccessfully tried to abduct a fourteen year old girl by claiming to be from the fire department. She thought it was strange that he was in plain clothes and driving a van. Luckily, her brother drove up and she left with him. The brother jotted down the van's license tag number. Their father was Chief of

Detectives with the Jacksonville Police Department. Another detective checked the registration and followed up with the owner, who told him the tag had been stolen. The man seen talking with the girl was later identified from an artist's sketch as Ted Bundy.

Two days later, Bundy kidnapped twelve-year old Kimberly Ann Leach from her school in Lake City, Florida. She was observed walking between school buildings. Witnesses last saw her being led to a white van by an angry-looking man whom they presumed was her father. He raped and murdered her and her body was found two months later near Suwannee River State Park. It was Bundy's final murder.

Bundy then returned to his apartment in Tallahassee, wiping it down for fingerprints. He abandoned the van and stole a car with which he was very familiar, a Volkswagen "Bug," similar to the one he utilized in the murders in the Northwest.

Heading west from Tallahassee, he was pulled over by a police officer in Pensacola, Florida who had called in the license number from the VW and learned the tag was stolen. After a violent struggle, the officer subdued and arrested Bundy.

By the time of his execution—ten years after his Florida convictions—Bundy had confessed to thirty-six murders. The actual number of his victims remains unknown and is suspected to be much higher.

It is commonly accepted that vans are particularly dangerous as they are often used in abductions. However, in Bundy's case, many of his abductions were made using a Volkswagen "Bug" or "Beetle" from which he had removed the front passenger seat to better conceal his victims.

The abductions and murders known or believed to be by Bundy in the states of Washington, Utah, Colorado and Idaho illustrate the enormity of his killing career and the compelling need for, and the failures of, the victims' personal, situational and residential security.

Here is a partial listing of Bundy's victims in the Northwest.

Washington:

Joni Lenz (18) was found beaten and raped with a metal rod broken off from her bed frame in the basement of a house she shared with other young women. She survived with brain damage and severe internal organ injuries. Bundy apparently entered and exited via an unlocked basement window.

Linda Healy (21) was abducted from her basement bedroom, where bloodstains were found. A basement door leading directly outside was unlocked and was determined to be the point of entry. She was never found. Bundy confessed to her murder.

Donna Manson (19) disappeared while walking on a college campus to a concert. She was not missed for several days, as she commonly and unexpectedly took off on hitchhiking "adventures." Bundy confessed to her murder.

Susan Rancourt (19) was last seen going to a meeting on campus. She worked a full time job in a nursing home and had a 4.0 GPA. Bundy confessed to her murder.

Brenda Baker (15) had run away from home. Her badly decomposed body was found in a state park and the cause of her death was not determined.

Georgianne Hawkins (18) was abducted from an alleyway after leaving her boyfriend's fraternity for her residence. When she was last seen, she had only about 40 feet to go. A scream was heard by a nearby house mother, but Georgianne had vanished. Bundy confessed to her murder.

Janice Ott (23) disappeared after being overheard talking to a man with a cast on his arm who said his name was "Ted," and that he needed help with his sailboat. Several other women had declined his request. Janice seemed annoyed, but went with him anyway and was never seen alive again. Bundy confessed to her murder.

Denise Naslund (18) was at a beach with her boyfriend. She left to go to the restroom and was seen there, but never made it back. Bundy confessed to her murder.

Skeletal remains of three of the Washington women were later found, and Bundy ultimately confessed that they were those of Georgianna Hawkins, Janice Ott and Denise Naslund.

Utah:

Nancy Wilcox (16) disappeared after being last seen riding in a VW similar to Bundy's. Her body was never found. Bundy confessed to her murder.

Melissa Smith (17) was the daughter of the Midvale, Oregon Chief of Police. She was last seen attempting to hitch a ride home after a night on the town. Bundy confessed to her murder.

Laura Aime (17) was last seen on Halloween leaving a cafe. She was found naked, raped, sodomized, strangled with her own stocking and beaten beyond recognition. Bundy confessed to her murder.

Debby Kent (17) disappeared a few hours after the botched DeRonch abduction in Salt Lake City. She was last seen leaving a school play. Screams were heard from the area of the parking lot, and a handcuff key was later found in the lot. She was never seen again - alive or dead.

Susan Curtis (15) was abducted from the campus of Brigham Young University while attending a youth conference. She was never seen again. Bundy confessed to her murder.

Nancy Baird (23) disappeared from a service station in Layton, UT where she worked. She was never found.

Colorado:

Caryn Campbell (23) left her boyfriend in the lobby of a hotel in Aspen to go to their room. She never returned. She was found near the hotel over a month later with severe head injuries and deep cuts on her body. Bundy was convicted of her murder, but escaped, eventually travelling to Florida.

Julie Cunningham (26) disappeared from the streets of Vail while walking to a nearby tavern to meet up with a friend.

Denise Oliverson (25) disappeared after leaving her home following an argument with her husband to go to her parents' house in Grand

Junction. She never made it there. Bundy confessed to her murder and said he dumped her body in the Colorado River.

Melanie Cooley (18) was last seen in Nederland, CO after walking away from her high school. Her body was found eight days later with head injuries, her hands bound and a pillowcase over her head. Bundy confessed to her murder.

Shelly Robertson (24) was last seen in Golden, talking to a man driving an old pickup truck at a gas station. Her body was found nude and decomposed near Vail, 500 feet inside an old mine entrance. Bundy confessed to her murder.

Idaho:

Lynette Culver (12) disappeared from her Junior High School playground in Pocatello. Bundy confessed to her murder and said he had thrown her body into the Snake River. It was never recovered.

Ted Bundy was executed in the Florida State Prison's electric chair on January 24, 1989—more than 15 years after he began his killing career. He was possibly the most notorious of the known American serial killers. There are, however, many more believed to still be "out there." Estimates of their numbers range from 35 to as many as 1700.

Ted Bundy was a successful serial killer because most women trusted him. He was successful because many women did not pay attention to their surroundings. He was successful because his victims let themselves become isolated. Yes, Ted Bundy was a "worst case scenario," but when your life is at stake, it's not a bad idea to examine your environment from a worst case scenario perspective.

References

Nash, R. (n.d.). Retrieved from http://tedbundy.150m.com/part1.html

Ted Bundy. (2013). *The Biography Channel website*. Retrieved 10:24, Oct 20, 2013, from http://www.biography.com/people/ted-bundy-9231165.

Combs, B. (n.d.). Retrieved from http://serialkillers.briancombs.net/1683/ted-bundy-may-be-implicated-in-santa-rosa-hitchhiker-murders/

Ted Bundy. (2013). *The Biography Channel website*. Retrieved 11:21, Nov 10, 2013, from http://www.biography.com/people/ted-bundy-9231165.

Ted Bundy: A case of schizoid necrophilia. Moes, Elizabeth C. 1. Melanie Klein & Object Relations, Vol 9(1), Jun 1991, 54-72.

Ted Bundy. (2013). *The Biography Channel website*. Retrieved 11:25, Nov 10, 2013, from http://www.biography.com/people/ted-bundy-9231165.

Gibson, D (2012). *Today in history: Would-Be Victim Escapes the Clutches of Ted Bundy*. Retrieved Nov 11 2013, from Examiner Web Site: http://www.examiner.com/article/today-history-would-be-victim-escapes-the-clutches-of-ted-bundy

Ted Bundy. (2013). *The Biography Channel website*. Retrieved 06:21, Nov 11, 2013, from http://www.biography.com/people/ted-bundy-9231165.

Meyers, A. (n.d.). The Ted Bundy Murders. *WCTV RSS*. Retrieved November 16, 2013, from http://www.wctv.tv/home/headlines/107475869.html?storySection=story

Fisher, J. (2013, January 4). Jim Fisher True Crime. *: Bite Mark Identification in the Ted Bundy Serial Murder Case*. Retrieved November 16, 2013, from http://jimfishertruecrime.blogspot.com/2013/01/bite-mark-identification-in-ted-bundy.html

Bell, R. (n.d.). Caught Again. *Ted Bundy — — Crime Library on truTV.com*. Retrieved November 16, 2013, from http://www.trutv.com/library/crime/serial_

The Predator: Ted Bundy. (n.d.). *The Predator: Ted Bundy*. Retrieved November 16, 2013, from http://tedbundy.150m.com/part5.html

Ted Bundy. (n.d.). *Ted Bundy*. Retrieved November 16, 2013, from http://www.crimemuseum.org/Ted_Bundy

Redwood, D. (2012, August 21). well said. - *Democratic Underground*. Retrieved November 16, 2013, from http://www.democraticunderground.org/1002

Active Serial Killers At Large Today | Serial Killers 2012 | Serial Killers Central. (n.d.). *Serial Killers Central*. Retrieved November 16, 2013, from http://www.serialkillerscentral.com/killers-at-large

3

RAPE AND SEXUAL ASSAULT

"It won't happen to me!"

"It" may be many things—robbery, physical assault, sexual assault, rape and even murder. All are classified as "violent crime." Violent crime is a fact of life in today's society. In 2011, the FBI estimated that over 1,200,000 violent crimes occurred nationwide. While aggravated assaults accounted for the highest number of violent crimes at 62.4%, robbery comprised 29.4%, forcible rape was 6.9% (over 82,000 in just one year), with murder making up 1.2% of these violent crimes. Sexual assault accounts for another 225,000 victims. The 2012 Violent Crime Report showed increases over 2011.

To believe "it" will never happen is like denying one could ever be injured or killed in a traffic accident, become seriously ill, lose a loved one from cancer—or get it yourself, break an arm or leg, or injure a knee or shoulder while engaging in sports or from a fall. All of these things will, and do, happen to someone, somewhere, and at some time.

Of all the "its" that might happen to a college woman, the most devastating, except for murder, is rape. This "it" is preventable.

Definitions and Statistics

What exactly is meant by "Rape" and "Sexual Assault?" The U.S. Department of Justice defines these terms thusly:

Rape: "The penetration, no matter how slight, of the vagina or anus with any body part or object, or oral penetration by a sex organ of another person, without the consent of the victim."

Sexual Assault: "Is any type of sexual contact or behavior that occurs without the explicit consent of the recipient. Falling under the definition of sexual assault are sexual activities as forced sexual intercourse, forcible sodomy, child molestation, incest, fondling, and attempted rape."

State statutes provide more details and similar definitions. They may specifically exclude physicians who are performing medically appropriate examinations from these definitions.

In the aggregate, the statistics of rape demonstrate that "it" really does happen, and often, to a whole lot of young women.

- More than 10% of American women will experience rape.
- 1 in 4 college women has been the victim of rape or attempted rape.
- About 90% of all campus rapes occur to victims who are under the influence of alcohol.
- Alcohol use at the time of the attack was found to be one of the four strongest predictors of a college woman being raped.
- Over 40% of college men admit to using coercive behavior to have sex, including ignoring a woman's protests, using physical aggression, and forcing intercourse.
- 15% of college men acknowledged that they had committed acquaintance rape.
- More than 10% admitted to using physical restraint to force a woman to have sex.
- Of the college women who have been raped, only 25% describe it as rape.
- College women are most vulnerable to sexual assault during the first few weeks of the freshman and sophomore years.
- Nearly 35% of rape-intended assaults result in completed rapes.
- 60% or more of the completed rapes occur in the victim's or rapist's residence.
- More than 75% of the men identified as rapists are an acquaintance, friend or boyfriend of the victim.
- Over 40% of victims are under the age of 18.
- About 80% of victims are under the age of 30.
- Less than half of rapes or sexual assaults are reported to law enforcement.

- Men are more likely than women to assume that a woman who drinks alcohol on a date is a willing sex partner.
- 40% of men who think this way also thought it was acceptable to force sex on an intoxicated woman.
- Most rapes occur on the weekend.
- More than 40% of college women who were raped were virgins at the time.
- One out of every 500 college students is believed to be carrying the HIV virus.
- Over 80% of rape survivors said the rape permanently changed them.

Can rape really forever change a woman's life? Here are a few more numbers to think about. Studies indicate that rape and sexual assault victims are: **3 times** more likely to suffer from depression, **6 times** more likely to suffer from post-traumatic stress disorder, **13 times** more likely to abuse alcohol, **26 times** more likely to abuse drugs, and **4 times** more likely to contemplate suicide.

Yes, it is unlikely that "it" will happen to you, but do you want to bet your life, or the rest of your life, on the possibility that it will not? The following chapters will address ways you can change the odds in your favor and make yourself a safer woman.

The Aftermath of Rape

The effects of a rape are far from over after the rapist has left. After a rape, it is imperative that the victim immediately seek medical attention. At some point, the police should be called. The victim must take the initiative and present herself for medical attention. If she does this first, and has not called the police, the medical facility will then contact the police. Many women are reluctant to take this first step, usually because of a fear of being judged, feeling ashamed or guilty, or because of psychological denial from shock.

Before a post-rape medical examination, the victim should not take a bath or shower, comb or brush her hair, change her clothes or shoes, and also, she should not douche. The medical facility will collect evidence by the means of a rape kit, any part of which the victim can refuse. This kit collects any semen left in the victim's vagina, other bodily fluids, and hair. The investigators will also look for other physical evidence, such as clothing, fibers, and scene evidence like grass or soil samples. They will likely scrape underneath the victim's fingernails, or take fingernail clippings to examine any skin or other residue from the attacker for DNA samples. Many successful criminal prosecutions have been made as a result of DNA matching.

Reporting rape is a personal decision, but there are many reasons to do so. The Rape, Abuse and Incest National Network (RAINN) reports that assisting in prosecution of her attacker helps to reestablish a sense of control in the life of the victim. Many women say it aided in their recovery.

In addition to any injuries that may have been suffered during the rape, there is also the potential (5-10%) of having been exposed to a sexually transmitted disease (STD) and a 1% chance of contracting HIV. Reporting the rape and getting examined will provide the opportunity to be tested for these diseases. That alone is a persuasive reason for getting medically examined.

Every year, thousands of women in the United States are raped. According to medical reports, the incidence of pregnancy for one-time unprotected sexual intercourse is 5%. This is a 5% chance that any given victim of reproductive age will become pregnant as a result of a rape. By applying the pregnancy rate to 64,080 women, the Rape and Incest National Network (RAINN), citing a study by physicians of the Department of Obstetrics and Gynecology of the Medical University of South Carolina, estimates that there were over **3,200 pregnancies,** as a result of rape, during the period researched.

If the woman is not already using contraceptives, a "morning-after" emergency contraceptive can be prescribed that reportedly has fewer side effects than the commonly prescribed morning-after pills, and is considered "safe" and reasonably effective if used shortly after the rape. After pregnancy—the attachment of the fertilized egg to the wall of the uterus—has occurred, the emergency contraception will not cause an abortion.

Once the physical injuries of rape have been addressed medically, there remain several emotional and psychological phases that will likely be suffered by the victim. She will first exhibit the acute phase of Rape Trauma Syndrome (RTS), which may typically last from a few days to a few weeks after the attack. A complete disruption of her life may, and probably will, be experienced. She may exhibit many different emotional responses, including shouting, swearing, inappropriate laughter, or even seem completely calm. She may appear "numb" from shock or disbelief. She may experience mood swings. There may be a disruption of normal sleeping or eating patterns. These are the victim's way of attempting to process the components of the experience.

Following the acute phase, there is a reorganization phase. During this, the victim will begin to reorganize her psyche and her life after the sexual assault. She learns to cope. The duration and effectiveness of this phase will depend upon her inherent coping mechanisms, support systems, existing life problems such as drinking or drug problems, relationship breakups, pre-existing emotional or psychological problems, and whether she has previously been assaulted.

She may have difficulty returning to pre-assault social patterns. She may become more distrustful toward men in general. She may move from the campus lodging or to a different location to "get away." She may drop out of school or change jobs.

Victims commonly experience denial during the reorganization phase of RTS. This may be useful in buying some time before trying to process and mentally resolve the trauma. Long term denial, however, is detrimental to their recovery.

It is not unusual for the victim to experience depression and a sense of guilt. She must be reminded by family and friends, or professional counselors if necessary, that she was not responsible for the violence she experienced. It was not she who perpetrated or voluntarily permitted the rape. It was the rapist who was responsible.

Long term effects of the rape may cause the victim to develop Post Traumatic Stress Disorder (PTSD), a condition usually associated with military war veterans, but also experienced by the victims of national disasters, severe accidents, and, of course, crime. It is most commonly associated with extreme or prolonged exposure to physical, emotional, or sexual abuse, but can be caused by a single sexual assault. PTSD symptoms include sleep disturbances, flashbacks or erratic mood swings.

Statistics from the U. S. Department of Justice, National Center of Public Analysis, and F.B.I. Uniform Crime reports show only 46% of rapes are reported to the police. This means that 54% of rapists get away scot-free, without even being identified. More alarmingly, only 12% of rapists are arrested, and only 9% are prosecuted for their crimes. Felony convictions occur in only 5 out of every 100 rapes, and only 3 out of every 100 rapists will ever spend a single day in prison. Even if prosecution is not successful, an encounter with law enforcement may deter the rapist from doing it again. Not reporting it may only encourage him to rape again.

Lack of Consequences

Lack of consequences for the rapist can be devastating to the victim. In April, 2006, Indiana University Freshman, Margaux J., was in and out of consciousness from intoxication when she was raped by another student living on the same floor in their dorm. Two administrators running the campus investigation believed her accusations and found that the rapist was "responsible" for "sexual contact" with her. The penalty? A suspension of a single summer semester for the rapist, despite his having a record of two prior campus offenses. His infractions included drinking alcohol in his dorm and punching another student in a fight following which he was investigated for criminal battery.

Margaux was furious. She wrote to the college, as did her father, and eventually the rapist was suspended for two additional semesters. Margaux finally had enough and dropped out of school. As she was admittedly highly intoxicated at the time of the rape, and was sometimes unconscious during the rape, her statement that, "Apparently, at Indiana (University), it's not rape when you have sex with someone who cannot give consent" seems entirely valid.

Margaux's experience is far from unusual. The Center for Public Integrity's year-long investigation found that students who are "deemed responsible" for alleged sexual assaults on college campuses can face little or no consequences for their actions, despite the devastation to the victims' psyches and lives. Lack of support on college campuses compounds the trauma. The Center reports that as many as 75% to 90% of all disciplinary actions for sexual assault amounted to minor sanctions: reprimands, counseling, suspensions, community service, alcohol treatment, and/or social probation. This is a factor in the decision whether or not to report the rape. Reporting it has benefits but also potential unpleasant social ramifications. Not reporting it allows the rapist to go on his way, unidentified, without consequences, perhaps to do it again. If he has been confronted by the police, it may deter him from repeating the offense.

False Rape Allegations

Sometimes, the report of a young college woman that she has been raped or sexually assaulted is not believed by school authorities and is considered to be a "false allegation."

There are grossly inconsistent statistics of false rape allegations. The Violence Against Women journal conducted a study and issued a report, "False Allegations of Sexual Assault: An Analysis in Ten Years of Reported Cases," finding that the seven examined studies from the years 1977 to 2006 had false reporting rates of 2.1 percent to 10.9 percent. That study also was highly critical of offering or using polygraph exams on alleged rape victims, calling it an "intimidation tactic that frequently persuades already hesitant rape victims to drop out of the criminal justice process." It also notes that the 2005 reauthorization for the Violence Against Women Act provides that any state using polygraphs on sexual assault victims may lose its eligibility for certain grants and that many states have passed laws against the use of the polygraph in determining appropriateness of charges in a sexual assault case.

In its 1995 Uniform Crime Reports, the U.S. Department of Justice, Federal Bureau of Investigation, came up with the figure of 8% of reported rapes as "unfounded," declining to use the word "false."

Because authorities sometimes doubt a victim's credibility, a legitimate rape may result in a lack of consequences, and cause other rapes to go unreported.

There appears to be little doubt that false rape allegations are indeed made, and for a variety of reasons. One study, with 45 cases of proved false rape allegations, led to the conclusion that false charges were motivated by the complainant to provide an alibi. An alibi could explain things such as, a sexually transmitted disease or pregnancy. The false claim might also be a means of gaining revenge against a male who has offended her, or a way to seek attention and/or sympathy.

False rape allegations can bring terrible consequences to the accused. In Ohio, a man was serving a long sentence for rape in spite of the absence of any physical evidence connecting him to the crime. According to a *Cleveland Plain Dealer* editorial supporting an expedited parole hearing, the inmate passed a voice stress test while asserting his innocence. In addition, the victim had repeatedly failed the same test, and the victim's former boyfriend, "has come forward to say she has a history of self-mutilation in attempts to gain attention." According to the paper, the victim claimed that, "she actually died during the attack and was brought back to life by Snow White." The editorial suggested that she may be an "unreliable reporter."

It is fortunate that her "unreliability" was belatedly discovered, but unfortunately not before an innocent man went to prison.

Making Changes to the "Rape Culture"

After coming under fire, colleges are attempting to implement changes in what has been called the "Rape Culture" on campuses. On April 4, 2011, the U.S. Department of Education's Office of Civil Rights (OCR) issued a "Dear Colleague" letter, a 19-page policy memo that was sent to deans and administrators across the country. It laid out colleges' responsibilities regarding preventing and addressing sexual harassment and assault under Title IX, the 1972 Gender Equity in Education Act. Most notable was a clear directive about the standard of proof for sexual misconduct. For decades, many schools had used a "clear and convincing" standard, requiring a panel to find it "highly probable or reasonably certain" that harassment or violence occurred before ruling in favor of a victim. But the government (Federal and State) requires only a preponderance of evidence in a civil rights dispute, that is, it must simply be more likely than not that the act took place. Schools must do the same, the letter said, regardless of what a police investigation might discover. Criminal conviction requires proof "beyond a reasonable doubt" as opposed to "preponderance of evidence" in a civil trial.

Even prior to the DOE's 2011 letter, student and faculty activists were pushing for change by invoking the Clery Act which requires schools to issue timely warnings about Clery Act crimes which pose a serious or ongoing threat to students and employees. Schools are to devise an emergency response, notification and testing policy, and enact policies and procedures to handle reports of missing students.

Title IX, of the Education Amendments of 1972, protects people from discrimination based on sex in education programs or activities which receive Federal financial assistance. It has been used, along with the Clery Act, as the basis for federal complaints by women at such diverse institutions as; University of California— Berkeley, University of Virginia, University of North Carolina, University of Maryland, Occidental College, Harvard University and Law School, Emerson College, Oklahoma State University, and George Washington University. Additionally, Stanford, University of Montana and University of Notre Dame have begun overhauls of their sexual assault policies as a result of the Clery Act and Title IX complaints. Other schools feeling the effects of such complaints are Yale University (hit with a $165,000 fine for failing to report campus sexual assaults in 2001 and 2002), Swarthmore College, University of Southern California, and Dartmouth College.

Amherst College is also making big changes in its sexual assault response programs after a student who said she was raped and was subsequently discouraged by school authorities from reporting it, published a 5,000 word, first-person account of her ordeal in the school newspaper. Her harrowing story begins with this:

"When you're being raped, time does not stop. Time does not speed up and jump ahead like it does when you are with friends. Instead, time becomes your nemesis; it slows to such an excruciating pace that every second becomes an hour, every minute a year, and the rape becomes a lifetime. On May 25, 2011, I was raped by an acquaintance in Crossett Dormitory on Amherst College campus."

Florida State University has developed a Victim Advocacy Program, which provides a multitude of services to rape and sexual assault victims ranging from 24 hour immediate post-assault crisis assistance through helping with any subsequent judicial process. Also, since 2009, sexual violence prevention training for FSU men in fraternities has been part of the bylaws of The Office of Greek Life. In the past year, workshops presented by peer educators detailing the issues of rape and sexual assault have been expanded to include women in the Greek system.

Why are changes so desperately needed? A persuasive argument for change from the website Feministing.com is the statement by one of its staffers, "Alexandra," about what the site calls "the prevalence of sexual violence on college campuses, and the shameful lack of support survivors tend to receive from campus administrations and even the federal government." Alexandra said,

"When someone attempted to rape me my freshman year, I asked my college, Yale University, for help, but instead I was basically advised to keep quiet. I shouldn't formally report the assault, I was told. Despite my clear and repeated, 'No,' school administrators cast the whole event as a misunderstanding among friends. In short, I was told to be a good girl. And for four years, I listened."

The increased awareness and proactivity by colleges and universities is certainly a most welcome development, but it should not be viewed as the definitive solution to the issue of sexual violence toward women. Individual behavior will continue to be the main component in rape and sexual assault, and their prevention.

Post-Rape Suicide

Post-rape harassment by peers may push a victim "over the edge" and into suicide.

One night in November, 2011, a Canadian 15 year old, Rehtaeh Parsons, was gang-raped at the home of one of her friends. One of the boys took a photo of her during the rape. He distributed the photo to everyone in the school and the community, and it went viral.

The boys had already manufactured a "slut" story, and that pejorative term stuck. Rehtaeh was, thereafter, considered as such by her peers. Her mother didn't hear of the assault until days after it happened when Rehtaeh broke down crying at home. It was too late for a rape kit. The boys were not interviewed by the Royal Canadian Mounted Police (RCMP) until much time had passed. The authorities dropped their investigation a year later without charges, but reportedly have now reopened it. The RCMP took no action with regard to the distribution of the photo, despite its dissemination constituting child pornography. The reason given was that they could not prove which one of the boys took the picture.

During the investigation, Rehtaeh experienced anger and depression, and was hospitalized on one occasion. She moved to another city to avoid peer harassment that lasted for nearly two years. The harassment included many text messages asking to have sex with her and still calling her a "slut" and a "whore."

Rehtaeh subsequently hanged herself in early 2013, but did not immediately die. After three days, she was taken off life support and perished.

After a public outcry, appeals were made to the hacker group, "Anonymous," which solved the case in two hours, identifying all four young men, as well as witnesses to the crime. The RCMP received heavy criticism for its earlier handling of the case.

In a recent Rolling Stone Article, "Sexting, Shame & Suicide" (Issue 1192 - page 48) which addresses, among other similar tragedies, Rehtaeh's rape and death, author Nina Burleigh reports that the RCMP, in August 2013, has finally charged two 18 year-old boys with disseminating child pornography (but not with rape).

One can wonder if Rehtaeh might not have taken her own life had she felt the authorities were appropriately dealing with the crime.

Who are the Rapists?

Serial killers have a starring role in Chapters 1 and 2, even though, statistically, the serial killer is the least likely predator to attack you. They have been examined in some detail because an encounter with one will most likely prove fatal to you. If one of them should succeed in abducting you, there is little chance you will survive.

The abductor rapist may not kill you, but, as Elizabeth Smart said, you may wish you were dead.

More commonly, the rapist will be, as statistically demonstrated, a friend, acquaintance or date, and the rape will most likely take place in his room/apartment or yours. By allowing yourself to become inattentive, intoxicated, or both, you greatly increase the risk that you will become a rape victim. Your defense must be against any potential murderer, rapist and abductor. That defense must include alcohol awareness. Do not forget: At least 50% of college students' sexual assaults are associated with alcohol use.

There is little you, as women, can do to change men's drinking practices, but you can certainly take control of yours. That is the first part of your defense. The next chapter will help you achieve that goal. If you fail to take control, you will be placing yourself in a dangerous environment with less than your full attention available to keep yourself safe and the monsters away.

References

Federal Bureau of Investigation. (2012, August 6). *FBI*. Retrieved November 16, 2013, from http://www.fbi.gov/about-us/cjis/ucr/crime-in-the-u.s/2011/crime-in-the-u.s.-2011/violent-crime/violent-crime

Federal Bureau of Investigation. (2013, May 7). *FBI*. Retrieved November 16, 2013, from http://www.fbi.gov/about-us/cjis/ucr/crime-in-the-u.s/2012/preliminary-annual-uniform-crime-report-january-december-2012

Statutes & Constitution :View Statutes : Online Sunshine. (2013, November 16). *Statutes & Constitution :View Statutes : Online Sunshine*. Retrieved November 16, 2013, from http://www.leg.state.fl.us/Statutes/index.cfm?App_mode=Display_Statute&Search_String=&URL=0700-0799/0794/Sections/0794.011.html

Rape Statistics. (n.d.). *Statistic Brain RSS*. Retrieved November 16, 2013, from http://www.statisticbrain.com/rape-statistics/

Statistics about Sexual Assault and College Campuses. (n.d.). *Statistics about Sexual Assault*. Retrieved November 16, 2013, from http://www.slc.edu/offices-services/security/assault/statistics.html

RAINN. (n.d.). Campus Safety | RAINN | Rape, Abuse and Incest National Network. *Campus Safety | RAINN | Rape, Abuse and Incest National Network*. Retrieved November 16, 2013, from http://www.rainn.org/public-policy/legislative-agenda/campus-safety

One In Four USA. (n.d.). Sexual Assault Statistics. *One In Four USA*. Retrieved November 16, 2013, from http://www.oneinfourusa.org/statistics.php

Connection. (n.d.). Rape Statistics. *Rape Statistics*. Retrieved November 16, 2013, from http://www.crisisconnectioninc.org/sexuala

Victim Services. (n.d.). Crime Victim Services (CVS). *Crime Victim Services (CVS)*. Retrieved November 16, 2013, from http://www.crimevictimservices.org/page/s

Ph. D, B. C. (n.d.). Rape and Sexual Assault Statistics Report. *Rape and Sexual Assault Statistics Report*. Retrieved November 16, 2013, from http://www.nmcsap.org/statistics.html

Resources. (n.d.). *For victims of sexual assault and sexual abuse Advocacy Support Center Elizabethtown Kentucky KY*. Retrieved November 16, 2013, from http://advocacysupportcenter.com/article-whattodo.asp

Larson, N. (2011, December 5). After Rape, Getting a Medical Exam is Essential. *About.com Women's Health*. Retrieved November 16, 2013, from http://womenshealth.about.com/lw/Health-Medicine/Womens-Health/After-Rape-Getting-a-Medical-nbsp-Exam-is-Essential.htm

MM, H., HS, R., & DG, K. (n.d.). Rape-related pregnancy: estimates and descriptive characteristics from a national sample of women. *NCBI*. Retrieved November 16, 2013, from http://www.ncbi.nlm.nih.gov/pubmed/8765

Emergency Contraception for Rape Survivors. (2007, November 1). *Center for Reproductive Rights*. Retrieved November 16, 2013, from http://reproductiverights.org/en/document/emergency-contraception-for-rape-survivors

Professor Blogs. (2004, December 9). CrimProf Blog. *CrimProf Blog*. Retrieved November 16, 2013, from http://lawprofessors.typepad.com/crimprof

Fluker, S. (2013, September 19). Survey seeks female opinion on sexual violence. *FSView*. Retrieved November 16, 2013, from http://www.fsunews.com/article/20130919/FSVIEW1/130919005/Survey-seeks-female-opinion-sexual-violence

Waugh, D. (2013, April 12). Rehtaeh Parsons Rape Case Solved By Anonymous in Less Than 2 Hours Despite "No Evidence". *PolicyMic*. Retrieved November 16, 2013, from http://www.policymic.com/articles/34491/rehtaeh-parsons-rape-case-solved-by-anonymous-in-less-than-2-hours-despite-no-evidence

Burleigh, N. (2013, September 17). Sexting, Shame and Suicide. *Rolling Stone*. Retrieved November 16, 2013, from http://www.rollingstone.com/culture/news/sexting-shame-and-suicide-20130917

4

ALCOHOL FACTS

Alcohol is the single greatest hazard to the safety and well-being of college students!

Here are the justifications for that statement:

Consequences of College Drinking

About four out of five college students drink alcohol. About half of the college students who drink do it by way of binge drinking (more on that later). Here are the results:

Injury: Nearly 600,000 students between the ages of 18 and 24 are unintentionally injured under the influence of alcohol.

Death: 1,825 college students between the ages of 18 and 24 die from alcohol-related unintentional injuries, including motor vehicle crashes.

Assault: Almost 700,000 students between the ages of 18 and 24 are assaulted by another student who has been drinking (this includes guy on guy assaults).

Sexual Abuse: 97,000 students between the ages of 18 and 24 are victims of alcohol-related sexual assault or date rape (you've seen this already in Chapter 3).

Unsafe Sex: 400,000 students between the ages of 18 and 24 had unprotected sex and more than 100,000 students between the ages of 18 and 24 report having been too intoxicated to know if they consented to having sex.

Academic Problems: About 25 percent of college students report academic consequences of their drinking, including missing class, falling behind, doing poorly on exams or papers, and receiving lower grades overall.

Health Problems/Suicide Attempts: More than 150,000 students develop alcohol-related health problems, and between 1.2 and 1.5 percent of students indicate that they tried to commit suicide within the past year due to drinking or drug use.

Drunk Driving: 3,360,000 students between the ages of 18 and 24 drive under the influence of alcohol.

Vandalism: About 11 percent of college student drinkers report that they have damaged property while under the influence of alcohol.

Property Damage: More than 25 percent of administrators from schools with relatively low drinking levels and over 50 percent from schools with high drinking levels say their campuses have a "moderate" or "major" problem with alcohol-related property damage.

Police Involvement: About five percent of four-year college students are involved with the police or campus security as a result of their drinking, and 110,000 students between the ages of 18 and 24 are arrested for an alcohol-related violation such as public drunkenness or driving under the influence.

Alcohol Abuse and Dependence: According to questionnaire-based self-reports about their drinking in the past twelve months, 31 percent of college students met criteria for a diagnosis of alcohol abuse and six percent for a diagnosis of alcohol dependence.

Alcohol Poisoning: This kills about thirty-six college students each year.

Emergency room treatment: One in three 18-24 year-olds each year who were admitted to an emergency room for serious injuries were intoxicated.

Fatal traffic crashes: One-half of all involving 18-24 year-olds also involved alcohol.

This is certainly not why you came to college.

40

It sometimes begins before young people ever enter college. Many students arrive on campus with established drinking habits. During any given month, more than a quarter of underage persons (ages 12-20) used alcohol, and binge drinking among the same age group was just slightly less than that number. Nearly three quarters of students have consumed alcohol (more than just a few sips) by the end of high school, and more than a third have done so by eighth grade. Drinking is a habit that will continue into college, and may get even worse because the college environment can exacerbate the problem. Home supervision has effectively ended, and peer pressure may increase.

It is a fact of life that the majority of college students consume alcohol. About half of them report binge drinking in the past two weeks. Abusive and underage college drinking are significant public health problems. They take an enormous toll on the intellectual and social lives of students on campuses across the United States. Drinking has become something that students often see as a normal part of college life. Virtually all college students experience the effects of college drinking, either directly or vicariously, and nearly every college student knows something about alcohol consumption and that its effects sometimes get out of control. They all know that drinking will cause one to become happy at first, then become a little silly and do things they wouldn't do if stone-cold sober, and that if they drink too much, they will begin to feel not so good or even really, really bad. Even if they don't drink, they probably have seen it in others.

This begs the question: Why DO you drink? Is it to be sociable? Is it to feel good and relax from the stress of a school week? To get just a little drunk? To get obviously drunk? To get "falling down" drunk? To become unconscious and pass out? Everyone who has been there and done that knows that being really drunk is no fun at all. Given this, why does it happen? The author suggests that inexperience with alcohol and lack of awareness of the way it is processed in your body are the primary culprits. So, let's work on that.

What Happens When Alcohol Enters the Body?

Once swallowed, alcohol enters the stomach and the small intestine, where it is carried to the bloodstream (and, of course, to the brain). It is metabolized by the liver. Generally, the liver can process one ounce of alcohol per hour—a Blood Alcohol Content (BAC) of .015%. Drinking more than can be metabolized leads to intoxication, producing effects that are sometimes quite serious.

Women, drinking the same amount as men, will get intoxicated faster and more intensely. Some of this has to do with the proportion of the body's water content, which is greater in men. Some of it is because women, having less of the enzyme that breaks down alcohol in the stomach, will absorb, through the small intestine, up to 30% more alcohol than men of the same height and weight, drinking the same amount of alcohol. This disparity will be even greater with men who are larger than the woman. Therefore, as alcohol is metabolized at about .015% per hour by the liver for both genders, each drink consumed by the average woman will be equal to almost two drinks by the average man.

Think of it in terms of two pails of water of different size. If you drop the same amount of alcohol in both pails, the smaller one will have a greater concentration of alcohol.

Because of all the above, your date, boyfriend, or casual acquaintance may still be relatively sober when you are quite drunk. After an evening of going drink for drink, you will be about twice as intoxicated as he will be. That's a very risky situation.

The Effects of Gender on Intoxication

Using the www.globalrph.com/bac.cgi BAC calculator, here are the approximate results of Dick and Jane drinking the same amount of alcohol in 1-1/2 ounce doses (the typical "shot") of 80 proof liquor or 12 ounce glasses, bottles or cans of 5% beer. Dick weighs 180 pounds and Jane weighs 125 pounds. Because of the variables involved, the BAC levels have been rounded to one hundredths.

Dick weighs 180 pounds and Jane weighs 125 pounds

1 drink in 1 hour: Dick = **.01%**Jane = **.03%**

2 drinks in 1 hour: Dick = **.04%**Jane = **.08%**

3 drinks in 1 hour: Dick = **.06%**Jane = **.12%**

4 drinks in 2 hours: Dick = **.07%**Jane = **.15%**

5 drinks in 3 hours: Dick = **.08%**Jane = **.18%**

To demonstrate the gender factor, let's assume Dick and Jane each weigh 150 pounds.

Dick and Jane both weigh 150 pounds

2 drinks in 2 hours: Dick = **.03%**Jane = **.05%**

3 drinks in 3 hours: Dick = **.04%**Jane = **.07%**

4 drinks in 2 hours: Dick = **.09%**Jane = **.12%**

6 drinks in 3 hours: Dick = **.14%**Jane = **.19%**

Jane is still going to get significantly more intoxicated than Dick even if they weigh exactly the same. In order for both to maintain the same BAC with the same number of drinks in a given time, Dick would have to weigh 125 pounds and Jane 160 pounds or other equivalent weight differences.

As demonstrated above, if Jane weighs more than 125 pounds, her BAC levels for each drink consumption scenario given above will be less, but not by much. Compare Jane's levels as shown above at 125 pounds and at 150 pounds. It's not fair, Ladies, but it is what it is.

It is critical that young women understand this disparity, and that they simply cannot go drink for drink with the boys without becoming significantly more intoxicated than they do, possibly leading to alcohol poisoning and becoming vulnerable to sexual assault or rape.

Compare Jane's BAC levels with those shown below (BAC Range and Physical/Mental Effects).

BAC Range and Physical/Mental Effects

The effects of alcohol intoxication may vary slightly from individual to individual. Some may become intoxicated at lower BAC levels than others.

If your friend begins to develop signs of significant intoxication, it is time to consider calling for medical intervention. You do not know if she will continue to become more intoxicated, even if she has quit drinking.

BAC Levels in percentages: (Compare to Dick's and Jane's BAC levels)

.02 Reached after approximately one drink; light or moderate drinkers will feel some warmth and relaxation.

.04 Most people feel relaxed, talkative, and happy. Their skin may flush.

.05 You will begin to feel noticeable changes. Lightheadedness, giddiness, lowered inhibitions, and less control of thoughts may be experienced. Your restraint and judgment are lowered and your coordination may be slightly altered.

.06 Your judgment is somewhat impaired. Normal ability to make a rational decision about personal capabilities is affected. Your driving ability is significantly reduced. <u>This is a pretty good time to stop drinking.</u>

.08 You will now be experiencing definite impairment of muscle coordination and a slower reaction time. It is now <u>illegal to drive</u> in virtually all states. You may have feelings of numbness of the cheeks and lips. Your hands, arms and legs may tingle and then feel numb. <u>You should stop drinking, now.</u>

.10 You have become clumsy and your speech may be slurred. There is a clear deterioration of reaction time and muscle control. <u>Stop drinking, NOW.</u>

.15 Your balance and movements are definitely impaired. This is "falling down drunk." The equivalent of a half-pint of whiskey is in your bloodstream. If you can make yourself vomit, do it. <u>Do NOT have any more drinks!</u>

.17 You are probably feeling anxious and restless. Your judgment and perception are severely impaired. <u>Now is the time to consider medical intervention</u>, especially if you have been drinking non-standard drinks, or have been consuming more than one per hour, or you have stopped drinking but feel like you are getting even more intoxicated. Try to vomit. Someone should at least call 800-222-1222 for rerouting to your local Poison Control Center. If that fails, call 911. Unless you have quit drinking an hour or so ago, you are at significant risk of becoming alcohol poisoned.

.20 Your motor and emotional control centers in your brain are significantly affected. Your speech is severely impaired; you will stagger, have loss of balance and may be experiencing double vision. You are lapsing into alcohol poisoning. <u>Someone should **call 911, immediately!**</u>

.25 All of your mental, physical and sensory functions are severely impaired. You are at great risk of choking from vomiting and of serious injury from falls or other accidents. This was an emergency .05% ago. You are now suffering from alcohol poisoning. <u>**Your**</u>

friends must not wait any longer to call 911 for help! (Please note that 6 drinks in two hours puts the 125 pound Jane at this level)

.30 You may be in a stupor: (Miriam-Webster Medical Dictionary) "...a chiefly mental condition marked by absence of spontaneous movement, greatly diminished responsiveness to stimulation, and impaired consciousness." You have little or no comprehension of where you are. You may pass out suddenly and be difficult to awaken. **This is long past the time someone should have called 911.**

.35 You may lapse into a coma. This is the level of surgical anesthesia. If you are not in the hospital by now, it could be too late. **There is a high probability you will die.**

When a Drink is Not a "Drink"

Compounding the problem is that a drink is not necessarily a "drink." The "Standard Drink" is a typical bottle or can of beer, a glass of wine, or liquor drink (mixed drink or straight liquor). This is sometimes called a "unit." Each "standard" drink contains virtually identical amounts of pure alcohol.

All drinks are not created equal. Beer, in the same size bottles or cans, can range from about 5% alcohol (a "Standard Drink") to as much as 12% in some malt beers. That is more than two standard drinks in one bottle or can. Many other drinks have alcohol concentrations well above the "standard" drink, including Margarita, Gimlet, Old Fashion, Dry Martini, Manhattan, Rob Roy and Frozen Daiquiri.

Long Island Iced Tea is very far from being a standard drink. It may be the equivalent of as many as five standard drinks. Here is what's in it: Vodka, Tequila, Rum, Gin and Triple Sec. Even if you nurse it for two or three hours, just one will get your Blood Alcohol Content (BAC) quite elevated. Drink two of them, and you'd better have a safe ride home and assistance with walking and getting safely into your residence. You'd also better have a female friend stay with you to watch for symptoms of alcohol poisoning (see below). As an example, if you weigh 140 pounds, take two hours to drink one Long

Island Iced Tea, and it is the equivalent of only eight, rather than ten, "units," you will have a greatly elevated BAC of .13% or higher.

Here is another BAC calculator from the Ohio University Police Department (http://www.ou.edu/oupd/bac.htm). Enter your weight and gender, number of drinks over what period of time, plug in your favorite drink and see your probable BAC. You will likely be surprised, if not shocked, at the result.

The bottom line is that having one standard drink per hour will allow you to metabolize most (but not all) of it before you have your next drink. Two drinks per hour will leave a little over one drink still in you, and your BAC will begin to rise. Four drinks in two hours will raise it even more. If you are drinking beverages with more alcohol than the "standard" alcohol content, your blood alcohol levels will rise even faster. Check the BAC Calculator again after reading the section below.

How to Maintain a Safe Blood Alcohol Level

How can you avoid these dire results? Here are some hints for maintaining a moderate blood alcohol concentration:

Know your limit

Check out the BAC calculator to enter your drinking habits. Know how many, over how many hours, you can drink of your favorite beverage to not exceed the BAC level that makes you uncomfortable just to think about it.

Eating food

If you eat while you drink (particularly meat and cheese), it will help slow the absorption of alcohol into your body.

Sip your drink

Don't gulp it.

Don't drink too much in a short period of time

Don't participate in "chugging" contests or other drinking games. You'll lose. Don't "do" shots—they will intoxicate you faster than mixed drinks.

Avoid bar specials

Avoid deals such as; "All You Can Drink" for a set price, "Four Drinks for Four Dollars," "Free Shots for Women," and "Dollar Doubles," all of which usually have a one to two hour time limit. They will psychologically lead you to drink more and at a quicker pace than you might by purchasing drinks at "retail." They want you there to attract the men drinkers. You are "bait." You will almost always drink too much in this environment. It is a very dangerous environment for young women.

Order a drink only when you really want one

If someone tries to force a drink on you, say "No." Space out your alcoholic drinks. One per hour, except for the high alcohol content of the drinks already described, should keep you out of trouble, unless you continue for several hours.

Keep active

Don't just sit around and drink.

Beware of unfamiliar drinks

It is difficult to space them properly.

Skip a drink now and then

Having a non-alcoholic drink or two—a soft drink or just the mix without the alcohol—between those containing alcohol will help keep your blood alcohol content level down.

Use alcohol carefully in connection with prescription medications

Ask your physician or pharmacist about any precautions or prohibitions (or look it up on-line) and follow any advice given.

Drinking too much alcohol is ALWAYS a bad idea. It invites the alcohol monster: To reiterate information previously given in Chapter 3, surveys of female college students found a significant relationship between the amounts of alcohol the women reported drinking each week and their experiences of sexual victimization, as well as having unprotected sex.

Alcohol Poisoning

Alcohol depresses nerves that control involuntary actions such as breathing and the gag reflex (which prevents choking). It is serious business if someone passes out. It is a huge red flag. It is very dangerous, and could prove to be fatal. In a state of severe intoxication, the stomach becomes irritated by the alcohol and will involuntarily try to expel it. That's why an intoxicated person may vomit. If the person is unconscious they may aspirate the vomit, choke, and die.

Symptoms and effects of alcohol poisoning include:

*Mental confusion, stupor, coma, the person cannot be awakened
*Slow breathing (fewer than 8 breaths per minute)
*Irregular breathing (10 seconds or more between breaths)
*Vomiting
*Hypothermia (low body temperature) possibly leading to seizures and death
*Slow reflexes
*Slurred speech, inability to effectively communicate
*Rapid pulse—sometimes a slow pulse
*Moist, clammy skin (similar to shock)
*Inability to walk
*Pale, blue colored skin
*Dehydration
*Stupor
*Unconsciousness
*DEATH

If you survive an alcohol overdose, you can still suffer irreversible brain damage.

Even after you have passed out, your blood alcohol level can continue to rise for another 45 to 60 minutes. That is why your friends must not assume that you will just sleep it off, and must take proactive steps (calling 911) to insure your safety.

What to Do for an Alcohol Poisoned Person

If someone you know has alcohol poisoning or you even <u>think</u> they do:

- Call 911 (in a sorority house, call the house mother).
- Stay with the victim. Never leave them unattended.
- Turn the person on their side to prevent choking if they vomit, or, if possible, seat them so that the head is lowered and they are leaning forward. **Do NOT let them lie face up!**
- Monitor the breathing levels. If you know CPR, be prepared to use it.
- Continue trying to revive the person if they have passed out.

Common sobering-up remedies such as drinking black coffee, taking a cold bath or shower, sleeping or walking it off do not work. The only things that will begin the sobering-up process are vomiting and time.

As crazy as it sounds, some people take alcohol enemas, sometimes called "butt chugging." Alcohol enemas are extremely dangerous. A University of Tennessee student who allegedly received an alcohol enema at his fraternity was taken to the hospital with a blood alcohol level of .40%. That's over five times the legal limit and is in what doctors call the "Death Zone" for alcohol poisoning. Another man, not a student and much older, died with a .45% BAC after his wife gave him a sherry wine enema.

Because the alcohol is absorbed more rapidly into the bloodstream by way of the colon than through the stomach and small intestine, the recipient gets drunk much faster by this method. To quote Atlanta gastroenterologist, Dr. Preston Stewart: "Our stomachs and livers have an enzyme known as alcohol dehydrogenase that breaks down ethanol to make it less toxic for our bodies. The lower gastrointestinal tract doesn't have that enzyme, so alcohol molecules are absorbed into the bloodstream through the lining of the colon." Eventually, the alcohol would still make its way to the liver, Dr. Stewart said, but the high alcohol content would overwhelm it.

Binge Drinking

This is the crux of the problem of over-drinking. By whatever name, it is simply the drinking of too much alcohol in too short a period of time. It is the most dangerous kind of drinking. By the time you start to feel drunk, there is still plenty of alcohol in your stomach and small intestine, and even if you stop drinking you will continue to get more intoxicated. This is how you slip into alcohol poisoning. This is why bar specials offered at a cheap price, and good only within limited time periods, are so dangerous.

Have you ever awakened in the morning with a really bad hangover after a lot of drinking the night before? Have you ever said to yourself or someone else, "I'm never going to do that again!" If so, MEAN IT! DON'T do it again.

Albert Einstein is famously quoted as giving this definition of insanity: ***"Doing the same thing over and over and expecting different results each time."*** If you continue to drink heavily you will not experience different results—with the exception that they may be worse results. The bottom line of social drinking is that being happy and feeling good is probably relatively safe. Nevertheless, other risks remain (See Chapter 5). If you drink to the point where you feel really bad, that is not okay.

Blackouts

One need not be in a non-functioning state of alcohol poisoning to black out. It can sometimes occur at lower alcohol levels and even to "social drinkers." It is not the same as "passing out" from too much alcohol.

Dr. D. F. Sweeney is an addiction physician who has written a book entitled: The Alcohol Blackout: Walking, Talking, Unconscious and Lethal, which examines this phenomenon. The title alone is scary. According to Dr. Sweeney, alcohol can block memory formation, suddenly and without warning. Self-control, inhibitions and decision-making processes disappear. Dangers are not recognized. Thoughts and actions are entirely impulsive. Some people black out often and others rarely do. Blackouts are unpredictable. Blackouts may last for a short time or for many hours. It may take very little alcohol to bring on a blackout. Blackouts can occur to first-time drinkers.

The person in a blackout does not necessarily appear abnormal—they can walk, talk, and even drive, but the alcohol prevents the formation of memories, thereby rendering the person essentially unconscious. Contrary to common belief, blackouts don't happen only to individuals who have had a lot to drink. Moderate drinkers can have blackouts as well. Dr. Sweeney makes the distinction between blackouts and alcohol-induced unconsciousness. The already discussed ways to keep your BAC at moderate levels have usually not been followed by the person suffering the blackout. He says, "Because of binge drinking, blackouts are epidemic on college campuses. Women are at greatest risk."

How to Drink Without Getting Drunk

Eat something first. Snack during the drinking, primarily proteins such as peanuts, cheese and meat. Slow down! Nurse your drinks. Don't do shots! Dilute the alcohol with water or a mix. After each alcoholic drink have one or two non-alcoholic drinks or just order the mix without liquor in it. As soon as you begin to feel intoxicated, stop for a while (at least an hour, and preferably longer) until you feel better.

You must be the boss of alcohol. Do not let alcohol be the boss of you. If alcohol becomes your boss, it will begin to own you and you will be well down the road to alcoholism and serious health and academic issues.

Driving Under the Influence of Alcohol (DUI)

One should NEVER drive after drinking ANY amount of alcohol. You will not know for sure when you have reached .08%, the DUI threshold. Being at or above this Blood Alcohol Content level is all the proof needed for you to be convicted of DUI. The author has been a Breathalyzer operator and instructor, and can say from experience that the chances of beating the machine are slim to none. Nevertheless, even if you are at a lower BAC but are driving erratically with liquor or beer on your breath, you will almost certainly be arrested if pulled over by the police. The chance of conviction is good, unless there is some other provable reason for the deterioration of your driving skills. That will require intervention by a skilled DUI attorney, and they are expensive. If you are arrested for DUI you will go to jail pending a very expensive trial. Your bond for release will be expensive. If you injure someone while DUI and are convicted, you may go to prison. If you kill someone while DUI and are convicted, you will go to prison for a long time. Florida DUI laws are in Chapter 316.193 of the Florida Statutes.

If you are in another state, check out its DUI laws. Chances are they will be similar.

When it is time for you to leave the place where you were drinking, such as a party or a bar, it is better that you not walk, even if you are not feeling intoxicated. If you absolutely must walk, have a couple of sober, or as nearly so as possible, friends go with you. If a trusted guy is along for the walk, it would be even better. Just a couple of drinks will cause you to be impaired to some degree, and you will be at risk. You should NEVER ride with a driver who has been drinking. The best way to get home is to call transportation services such as a taxi (always keep cab fare on you), or the free taxi that is sponsored by some universities (including FSU). If you try to go it on your own, your life could change forever in an instant.

Riding in Pickup Trucks

Even if the driver has not been drinking, never, ever, ride in the back of a pickup truck. If there is a crash, at a low speed, you will be thrown against the side of the bed or the back of the cab. At higher speeds, you can be catapulted out of the truck bed and hit the pavement, another car, or a fixed object. If you drive a pickup, never let anyone ride in the bed. From experience investigating these kinds of traffic accidents, you can be assured they result in injuries, usually serious, and many times in death. Although it may be legal for persons 18 and older to do so, it is a very, very dangerous thing to do.

References

Drinking. (2013, March 1). A Snapshot of Annual High-Risk College Drinking Consequences. *College Drinking: Changing the Culture*. Retrieved November 16, 2013, from http://www.collegedrinkingprevention.gov/

College Drinking. (n.d.). *NIAAA*. Retrieved November 15, 2013, from http://pubs.niaaa.nih.gov/publications/CollegeFactSheet/CollegeFactSheet.pdf

Ph.D, D. H. (n.d.). College Student Alcohol-Related Deaths: 36 or 1,400 Per Year?. *College Student Alcohol-Related Deaths: 36 or 1,400 Per Year?*. www2.potsdam.edu/handondj/driving issues/1127227453.html

Drinking Facts. (n.d.). *Drinking Facts*. Retrieved November 16, 2013, from http://www.brad21.org/facts.html

SADD Statistics. (n.d.). *SADD Statistics*. Retrieved November 16, 2013, from http://www.sadd.org/stats.htm

University. (n.d.). Alcohol & Your Body. *Brown University Health Education*. Retrieved November 15, 2013, from http://brown.edu/Student_Services/Health_Services/Health_Education/alcohol,_tobacco,_&_other_drugs/alcohol/alcohol_&_your_body.php

NIAAA. (n.d.). Alcohol and Women. *Alcohol and Women*. Retrieved November 16, 2013, from http://alcoholism.about.com/cs/alerts/l/blnaa10.htm

University of Notre Dame Division of Student Affairs. (n.d.). Differences Between Men and Women. *OADE University of Notre Dame*. Retrieved November 16, 2013, from http://oade.nd.edu/educate-yourself-alcohol/alcohol-and-women-critical-information/differences-between-men-and-women/

Blood Alcohol Calculator. (2012, November 13). *Blood Alcohol Calculator*. Retrieved November 16, 2013, from http://www.globalrph.com/bac.cgi

What's a "standard" drink?. (n.d.). *What's a standard drink?*. Retrieved November 16, 2013, from http://rethinkingdrinking.niaaa.nih.gov/whatcountsdrink/whatsastandarddrink.asp

Facts About Alcohol Poisoning. (2007, July 11). *Facts About Alcohol Poisoning*. Retrieved November 16, 2013, from http://www.collegedrinkingprevention.gov/otheralcoholinformation/factsaboutalcoholpoisoning.aspx

Effects of Increased BAC Levels on a Typical Person. (n.d.). *LEAD*. Retrieved November 15, 2013, from http://www.abc.ca.gov/FORMS/ABC627.pdf

What Is Alcohol Poisoning? How Dangerous Is Alcohol Poisoning?. (2011, February 3). *Medical News Today*. Retrieved November 16, 2013, from http://www.medicalnewstoday.com/articles/215627.php

Palmera. (2012, September 17). DisplayPhoneText("NNN-NNN-NNNN");(858) 481-4411Why CasaTreatmentsLocationAdmissions. *Casa Palmera*. Retrieved November 16, 2013, from http://casapalmera.com/signs-effects-of-alcohol-poisoning/

Wilson, J. (1970, January 1). Experts: Alcohol enemas 'extremely dangerous'. *CNN*. Retrieved November 16, 2013, from http://www.cnn.com/2012/09/26/health/alcohol-enemas

Binge drinking. (n.d.). *Binge drinking*. Retrieved November 16, 2013, from https://www.drinkaware.co.uk/understand-your-drinking/is-your-drinking-a-problem/binge-drinking

University. (2011, May 14). Social Drinkers Can Blackout Too. *About.com Alcoholism*. Retrieved November 16, 2013, from http://www.alcoholism.about.com/cs/college/a/blduke030214.htm

Blackouts and Alcohol Poisoning. (2009, November 11). *Promises Addiction Treatment Alcohol Drug Rehab Malibu*. Retrieved November 16, 2013, from http://www.promises.com/articles/alcoholabuse/blackouts-and-alcohol-poisoning/

Statutes & Constitution :View Statutes : Online Sunshine. (2013, November 16). *Statutes & Constitution :View Statutes : Online Sunshine*. Retrieved November 16, 2013, from http://leg.state.fl.us/Statutes/index.cfm?App_mode=Display_Statute&Search_String=&URL=0300-0399/0316/Sections/0316.193.html

Florida Drunk Driving Fines & Penalties. (n.d.). *dui.drivinglaws.org*. Retrieved November 16, 2013, from http://dui.drivinglaws.org/florida.php

5

"DATE RAPE" DRUGS

The rape of an intoxicated woman may be a crime of opportunity. The rape of a drugged woman is usually a crime of premeditation. Both are very wrong, and both are felonies.

While the terms "date rape" or "acquaintance rape" are widely used, it is wise to think of this as a "drug-facilitated sexual assault." That is the primary reason someone will spike your drink with a date rape drug.

General Effects of Drink Spiking

- Unconsciousness
- Decreased inhibitions
- Paralysis
- Inability to protect oneself
- Memory loss
- Nausea and vomiting
- Muscle spasms
- Poor coordination
- Feelings of euphoria
- Extreme sleepiness
- Respiratory complications, slurring of speech, and dizziness

What are Drink Spiking "Date Rape" Drugs?

The following is a list of commonly known and used date rape drugs. Becoming familiar with the names and common street names of these drugs is important and could one day save your life or a friend's. If you hear someone use any of these names other than "alcohol" in a drinking environment, beware! Better yet, LEAVE!

ROHYPNOL Nicknames: Circles, Forget Pill, La Rochas, Lunch Money, Mexican Valium, Mind Erasers, Poor Man's Quaalude, R-2, Rib, Roach, Roach-2, Roches, Roofies (probably the most common), Roopies, Rope, Rophies, Ruffies, Strip and Fall, and Whiteys. Rohypnol effects can be felt within 30 minutes of being drugged and last for several hours.

The **symptoms** of the person who has drunk something with Rohypnol in it may include looking and acting like someone who is drunk. She will have trouble standing, her speech will be slurred and she may pass out. The effects of Rohypnol can include nausea, lack of memory as to what happened while drugged, loss of consciousness, confusion, visual difficulties, dizziness, sleepiness, lowered blood pressure, stomach problems, and sometimes even **death**.

GHB Nicknames: Bedtime Scoop, Cherry Meth, Easy Lay, Energy Drink, G, Gamma-10, Georgia Home Boy, G-Juice, Gook, Goop, Great Hormones, Grievous Bodily Harm, Liquid E, Liquid Ecstasy, Liquid X, PM, Salt Water, Soap, Somatomax and Vita-G. GHB takes effect in about 15 minutes and can last 3-4 hours. Traces of GHB disappear from the body in 4 to 5 hours and may be difficult, if not impossible, to detect in the blood or urine after that time. It is extremely potent as an aphrodisiac and a small amount can have a large effect. It is very easy to overdose on it.

The **symptoms** of GHB include relaxation, drowsiness, dizziness, nausea, vision problems, loss of consciousness, seizures, loss of memory about what happened while drugged, breathing difficulties, tremors, sweating, vomiting, slow heart rate, dreamlike feelings, and sometimes **death**.

CHLORAL HYDRATE Nicknames: Mickey, Mickey Finn, Knock-Out drops.

The **symptoms** of chloral hydrate ingestion include confusion, convulsions, difficulty swallowing, severe drowsiness, hypothermia, nausea, vomiting, or severe stomach pain, shortness of breath, slow or irregular heartbeat, slurred speech, staggering, severe weakness, and possible death.

"MOLLY" is slang for pure "Ecstasy," or MDMA. The nickname is said to be short for "molecule." It is a relatively new compound, but its use is on the rise. The drug's popularity increased after the performer Madonna went on stage at a concert and shouted to the audience, "How many people in this crowd have seen Molly?"

Molly is extremely dangerous in high doses. It triggers a release of dopamine in the brain. Dopamine is the main hormone responsible for pleasure, and is why MDMA is often called the Love Drug. It is what makes users "high." They feel euphoria, intense physical pleasure, openness, emotional increase, and they may experience mild auditory and visual hallucinations. This drug is sometimes pure, but still dangerous. It may be cut with cheaper or harder drugs such as methamphetamine or heroin, making it even more dangerous. It can easily be mixed with drugs such as GHB. It is commonly mixed with marijuana and alcohol. Mixing drugs in this fashion intensifies the effect and greatly increases the risk of serious injury. Dopamine is also responsible for regulating body temperature, which will rise after taking MDMA, and may cause liver, kidney, and cardiovascular failure. Severe dehydration can result from the combination of the drug's effects and the crowded and hot conditions in which the drug is often taken. Some young people have literally danced themselves to death.

"EYE DROPS" is not the nickname of a drug such as the ones above, but literally, the contents of the small plastic bottles of eye drops that you buy at the grocery or drug store for relief of eye irritation. When mixed with alcohol, it can cause drowsiness, nausea, amnesia, and many of the other symptoms of date rape drugs. "Eye Drops" have been called the new Rohypnol. They are being used to spike victim's drinks in nightclubs and at parties, making them easy targets for robbers and rapists.

KETAMINE Nicknames: K, Special K, Vitamin K, Super Acid, Super C, Bump, Cat Valium, Green, Honey Oil, Special la Coke, and Jet. It is an anesthesia, mostly used in veterinary medicine. It has found its place as a club drug and can be in the form of a clear liquid or a white powder. It can cause confusion and disorientation, drowsiness, amnesia, temporary paralysis, and inability to speak. It can produce hallucinations and a feeling of complete sensory detachment that has been described as a near-death experience known as being "in the k-hole."

ALCOHOL—Along with the other drugs listed above, alcohol must also be considered a "date rape," "acquaintance rape," or "drug-assisted sexual assault" drug. It is the one most commonly used in sexual assaults and rapes. Any drug that affects judgment and behavior can put a person at risk for unwanted or risky sexual activity. Alcohol is clearly such a drug. When a person drinks too much alcohol, it's harder to think clearly, it's harder to set limits and make good choices, it's harder to tell when a situation could be dangerous, it's harder to say "No" to sexual advances, it's harder to fight back if sexual assault occurs, and it is possible to black out and to have memory loss. Unless someone has been keeping track of the number of drinks you've had, it can be difficult to know if you have alcohol poisoning or if your drinks have been spiked.

How to Guard Against Having Your Drink Spiked

- Don't accept drinks from other people. Not from anyone.
- If someone offers to get you a drink from the bar or a party, go with that person to order your drink. Watch the drink being poured and carry it yourself.
- Never leave your beverage unattended. Keep it with you at all times, even when you go to the bathroom. Cover it with your hand or a napkin if it is on the bar or a table.
- At a pub, bar, or club, accept drinks only from the bartender or server.
- When drinking, keep an eye on your friends and ask them to watch out for you.
- Open beverage containers (cans, bottles) yourself.
- Don't share drinks.
- Don't drink from punch bowls or other common open containers, as they may already have drugs in them.
- Don't drink anything that tastes or smells strange.

- Have a non-drinking friend with you to help make sure nothing happens.
- If you realize you left your drink unattended, pour it out.
- If you or someone else seems extremely intoxicated after drinking only a small amount of alcohol or a non-alcoholic beverage, the drink may have been spiked. Get help, immediately!

How to Tell if You May Have Been Drugged and Raped and What to Do

Most drugged victims don't remember being drugged or assaulted. You may not be aware of the assault until 8 to 12 hours after it occurred. Most of these drugs leave the body very quickly, and traces are gone after about 8 hours from ingestion (GHB after about four hours). Once a victim gets help, there may be no proof drugs were involved in the attack. There are, however, some signs that you may have been drugged and raped.

- You wake up feeling very hung over and disoriented, or having no memory of a period of time after your last drink
- You find that your clothes are torn or are not on right
- You feel like you had sex, but you cannot remember it

If you think you have been drugged or raped, get medical care right away. As discussed in Chapter 3, do not douche, bathe, wash your hands, change clothes, or eat and drink before you go to the hospital. If possible, do not urinate before reaching the hospital (they will want a urine sample to test for date rape drugs). Call the police from the hospital. Volunteer (and even ask) for a rape kit test to be performed. It is crucial that you be at least tested for STDs and HIV. If you are anywhere near the ovulation stage of your cycle, you must at least consider the potential benefit of an emergency contraceptive (which, as discussed in Chapter 3, will not cause an abortion if the fertilized ovum has attached to the placenta).

As also discussed in Chapter 3, post-rape feelings of shame, guilt, fear and shock are normal. Get counseling and treatment. A counselor can help you work through these emotions and begin the healing process.

Calling a crisis center or hotline is a good place to start. The National Assault Hotline telephone number is 1-800-656-HOPE (4673).

References

Palmera. (2012, September 17). *Casa Palmera*. Retrieved November 16, 2013, from
http://casapalmera.com/effects-of-drugs-used-in-drink-spiking/

Roofies. (n.d.). *Roofies*. Retrieved November 16, 2013, from
http://Web.jmu.edu/osasap/roofies.htm

Ph.D, N. B. (n.d.). Chloral Hydrate. *Doctors, Patient Care, Health Education,
Medical Research*. Retrieved November 16, 2013, from
http://www.pamf.org/teen/risk/drugs/daterape/chloralhydrate.html

Makarechi, K. (2012, March 26). Deadmau5 Slams Madonna Over 'Molly,' Ecstasy
Reference At Ultra Music Festival. *The Huffington Post*. Retrieved November 16,
2013, from http://www.huffingtonpost.com/2012/03/26/deadmau5--madonna-
molly-ultra-_n_1379437.html

"Molly," Powder or Crystal Form of MDMA, is Popular at Music Festivals. (n.d.).
The Partnership at Drugfreeorg. Retrieved November 16, 2013, from
http://www.drugfree.org/join-together/drugs/molly-powder-or-crystal-form-of-
mdma-is-popular-at-music-festivals

DEA - Get Smart About Drugs - A Resource for Parents from the DEA. (n.d.). *Get
Smart About Drugs*. Retrieved November 16, 2013, from
http://www.getsmartaboutdrugs.com/drugs/ecstasy_or_mdma.html?v=0&t=0&p=1
&f=0&df=0&dt=0

Bowman, C., & Joyce, L. (2010, July 22). Nightclubs keep an eye on new date rape
drug. - *Crime & Courts*. Retrieved November 16, 2013, from
http://www.iol.co.za/news/crime-courts/nightclubs-keep-an-eye-on-new-date-rape-
drug-1.1346460#.UdHzr_m1ExE

T, B. (2013, September 4). Basic Facts About Ketamine. *About.com Alcoholism*.
Retrieved November 16, 2013, from
http://www.alcoholism.about.com/od/lsd/a/Basic-Facts-About-Ketamine.htm

Date rape drugs fact sheet. (n.d.). *womenshealth.gov*. Retrieved November 16, 2013,
from http://www.womenshealth.gov/publications/our-publications/fact-sheet/date-
rape-drugs.cfm

6

PERSONAL SAFETY FOR COLLEGE WOMEN

It is unlikely anyone would deny that the world we live in is very unsafe. All one needs to do is read the headlines and watch the evening news. As they say in the news business, "If it bleeds, it leads." It leads a lot, and isn't letting up. The FBI reports that violent crime (murder, forcible rape, robbery and aggravated assault) increased by 1.2% from 2011 to 2012. That is a small percentage, but it represents big numbers.

Violent crime is not limited to the streets of big cities. It is a problem on college campuses as well. Averaging FBI crime data from 2008 through 2011, Business Insider magazine released a list of the top twenty-five most dangerous colleges. They were ranked based on a combination of violent crimes and property crimes, with violent crimes being weighted at 4 to 1 over property crimes. Here are numbers 1 through 5 and numbers 21 through 25:

#1 - University of California - Los Angeles with 49 Violent Crime Incidents (VCI)

#2—University of California—Berkeley with 38 VCI

#3 - Duke University—with 14 VCI

#4—Florida A&M University with 15 VCI

#5—Vanderbilt University with 11 VCI

#21—North Carolina Agricultural and Technical State University with 7 VCI

#22—State University of New York College—Buffalo with 8 VCI

#23—Arkansas State University—Jonesboro with 9 VCI

#24—University of California—Riverside with 11 VCI

#25—Florida State University with 26 VCI

Despite these alarming statistics, there are things you can do (and not do) that will reduce the chance of your becoming a victim. You have already read some of them in the preceding chapters. This chapter will give you even more to work with, in order to stay safe.

Professional Residential Security

If you live in a sorority house or apartment, professional security services will have a significant impact on increasing your personal safety. Most apartment complexes that cater to college students contract with private security firms. Most sorority houses at Florida State University have contracted for this service, but a few have not, apparently believing it is "too costly." Arguably, this is short-sighted, given Ted Bundy's history at FSU. If such a sorority should ever have a major incident, there is the very real possibility that litigation (a law suit) could follow. That would be costly not only in terms of money but also in the disruption of the residents' lives following the incident.

Legal liability can occur when there is foreseeability—the ability to anticipate—(Ted Bundy provided that), reasonable preventative measures were available (professional security accomplishes that), and such prevention was not implemented. Simply stated, if the responsible person knows about it, and it can be reasonably anticipated that someone could be hurt because of it, nothing is done to remedy it, and someone is indeed hurt; the responsible person and their company could face a law suit and a monetary judgment.

Professional security is effective because it is a deterrent to would-be criminals. Security's job is not to chase down and arrest bad guys, but rather to discourage the bad guys from even coming around. The security officer patrols the sorority house or other premises to see and to be seen. His or her duties are to look for anything that is out of the ordinary and take such action as might be necessary. This may include requiring unwanted visitors to leave the property, or calling the police for more serious matters.

Some sororities require that their security officers patrol only the exterior of the premises, while others include the common areas of the interior as well. The latter is a more complete method of security. First-floor doors and windows are checked for integrity from the inside as well as from the outside. Guests are monitored for behavior and reminded to leave at an hour set by sorority rules. Any disturbances inside the house can be overheard and dealt with. Residents with medical difficulties receive a quicker response, as the House Mother will be quickly contacted by the security officer. In both methods, the parking areas will also be patrolled, and, to the degree possible, residents will be escorted to and from their cars

Sorority sisters appreciate having professional security at their house. So do their parents. Perhaps the sorority residents who do not have a security officer at their house would not object to paying a little more in dues or house fees to have the benefit of this service.

Personal Residential Security

Many off-campus apartment buildings utilize the services of a professional security agency. Some do not. Having a security officer helps, but due to the size of many of these facilities, he or she cannot be in every location at any given time. The college woman therefore must take on additional responsibilities for her own safety and security. Here are some precautionary steps to take.

Pre-rental inspection of the apartment environment: Bad guys can hide in and behind bushes. Make sure any that are near the entry-way or the windows are well-trimmed and cannot conceal anyone from view.

Check to see if entryways and premises sidewalks are well-lit.

Find out if the outer doors are always kept locked. They should be made of solid core wood or metal, as should be the apartment doors. The locks and striker plates must be mounted securely.

The apartment doors should be equipped with a deadbolt. Ask the landlord or building manager if the door locks have been rekeyed after the last tenant moved out.

All windows and doors, particularly those on the first floor and those at fire escapes, should be equipped with locks to prevent entry from the outside. If the windows are equipped with security gratings, they should be operable from the inside in case of fire.

Make sure the apartment door has a peep-hole.

Assure that the apartment has a working smoke detector. There should be at least two emergency escape routes from the building for every room or apartment.

If you use a cell phone, check from the inside of the apartment to be sure you have a strong signal with no interference. If you choose to have a land-line telephone, is there a connection in the apartment for it?

Once in your new apartment, there are several things you can do to help assure you and your property stay safe.

Windows and doors: Always keep doors and windows to your apartment locked, especially when you are alone, sleeping, or the apartment is left unoccupied (even if only for a few minutes). If your windows are the sliding kind, put a length of dowel along the window track to prevent it from being opened if the lock should be forced or broken. Most burglaries involve unlocked doors, so locking up is the single most effective action you can take to reduce theft and prevent assault.

Keep first floor and other accessible windows closed and locked unless they are equipped with security gratings. If so, make sure the grate can be opened from the inside.

Do not leave the exterior doors of your building or your apartment doors unlocked or propped open. When entering or exiting, make sure all doors are securely locked. If you see a door that is not secure, lock it. Remember, this is how Ted Bundy got into the sorority house at FSU. Always keep your windows covered at night and leave lights on in two or more rooms.

Without delay, report such things as malfunctioning doors, windows, security gratings, lights, and overgrown shrubbery to the person responsible for maintaining your residence.

Strangers and visitors: Do not allow strangers into your building or apartment. If you see them wandering inside or loitering outside your house, dorm or apartment building, report them to the police or to security. If you have a visitor at the door, call out in a loud voice, "I'll answer it!" to imply that you are not alone. Observe visitors through your door peep-hole or window prior to opening the door. Have repair or service personnel show official identification and confirm their presence with the person requesting the service. Delivery persons should remain outside to await the person requesting the delivery.

Escort your guests into and out of the building. You are responsible for the conduct of your guests while they are present in your building. Individuals not living in your building may not have a sense of obligation to you, your property, or other residents.

Unwanted phone calls: Report all obscene or harassing phone calls to the police. If someone calls with the wrong number, never give the caller your name, address, or the number that they have called. A second wrong-number call may be inadvertent. A third wrong-number call from the same person is harassment. After the fourth, call the police. Your cell phone should show the caller's telephone number. If the number is blocked, don't answer the phone the first time.

Texts: If you receive a text message from a friend or relative asking you to meet them somewhere, call to verify that they sent the text. You are probably in their call list, and someone else could have their lost or stolen phone.

Police telephone number: Keep your local or campus police telephone number handy in case you need to report something. Program it into your cell phone, although in an emergency, you should always call 911.

Protect your identity: Do not use your first name on mailboxes or in telephone directories. Use your first initial only.

Never volunteer your name to a stranger. If a man asks you if you are "Jane Smith" just say "No." If you give your name, and he can identify the building in which you reside, it will be a simple task for him to check the names on the mailboxes to get your apartment number.

Leave a generic message on your answering machine. Don't give your name or imply you are away. Just say something like, "I can't come to the phone right now. Please leave a message."

Dangerous areas: Beware of deserted laundry rooms, common lounges, basements, parking garages, and elevators, especially late at night. If at all possible, use or enter these areas only when others are around.

Stairwells vs. elevators: Use the elevator rather than the stairwell, as you could be ambushed there. An elevator can also be risky. If an elevator stops for you and a stranger is in it, don't get on. If he holds the door for you, tell him thanks, but you are waiting for your boyfriend. If the elevator returns and he is still on it, don't enter unless he gets off and walks away. Look at his face. Don't smile. He will know you can identify him if he gets out of line.

If someone gets on who makes you feel uneasy, get off the elevator at once. Take the next one. Even if you are not uncomfortable, stand next to the control panel. If the guy gets at all inappropriate, or makes unpleasant remarks to you, immediately push the emergency alarm button and as many floor buttons as possible. Do not push the stop button. Try to keep him from reaching it. As soon as possible, get off, SCREAM and head for a safe place.

Valuables and money: In your apartment, keep valuables like currency, wallets, jewelry, and purses out of plain view. Do not leave valuables unattended in common areas such as laundry rooms and lounges.

Engrave property such as computers, stereos, and other electronic equipment with your driver's license number and state. This will aid in the recovery of your property if it is stolen. Do **not** use your name or Social Security number. Your campus police department may be able to suggest where you can rent or borrow an engraver. Many campuses, such as Florida State University, offer this

68

service for a small fee through the bookstore or campus police department.

Avoid carrying large sums of money on you. Open a savings or checking account rather than allowing large amounts of money to accumulate in your room.

Make sure your car is always locked and that any valuables left in it are locked in the trunk or placed out of view (the trunk is better). If the trunk is too full, or if you drive an SUV without a rear cargo cover, take your valuables inside.

Bicycles: If your bicycle must be stored or parked outside at your residence, make sure that it is secured to an immovable object with a chain or cable lock long enough to be looped through both the frame and the front wheel.

You should be alert to anything that seems even slightly "out of the ordinary" for the area or time of day in which it occurs.

Things to look out for and report (give a description if at all possible).

- Strangers entering your neighbor's room or apartment when it is unoccupied
- Strangers on your block trying doors to see if they are locked
- Screams heard anywhere, anytime may mean an assault or robbery is in progress
- The sound of breaking glass or other loud, explosive noises may mean an accident, burglary, vandalism or even a shooting
- Persons around bicycle racks carrying bolt cutters and tools
- A person running rapidly, especially if carrying something of value, could be leaving the scene of a crime.
- The sound of a crying baby may be a scam to get you outside. Do not go outside. This may be a serial killer's technique. Call 911 immediately.
- If all your exterior water faucets have been turned on, do not go out to check. It may be another serial killer trick. Call 911 and ask them to send an officer to watch while you turn them off.

While the situations described above could have innocent explanations, your police department would rather investigate possible criminal activities than be called after it is too late. Your call could save a life, prevent an injury, or stop a criminal act.

Personal Safety When "Out and About"

Parties, clubs and dating: The first rule of safety at a party or when clubbing is to be careful with your drinking. You know why - the chapter on alcohol covered this in detail.

Try not to go partying or clubbing alone. If you must, then before you leave your residence, make a plan to get home. Coordinate with friends and arrange transportation. If you do go alone, tell a sorority sister or friend where you are going and when you expect to be back. Let her know if your plans change.

Pay attention to what is happening around you. That's hard to do if you've had too much to drink. Try to attend parties with friends you can trust. Look out for each other.

Do not go to remote or private areas of the party. Do not go off alone with anyone at a fraternity party. Most fraternity brothers are nice guys, but they have been known to sometimes drink a lot, and they can lose their good judgment and self-control. Don't be around if that happens.

Repeat: DO NOT hang out alone with a guy or guys who have had a lot to drink. If you do, and if any of them show anger, jealousy, or possessiveness, or are becoming overly "friendly," get away from them. If any or all of them get "pushy," remember that "NO" means "NO!" Say it loudly. If he (or they) doesn't seem to get it and makes unwanted advances, scream for help. Respond physically if you need to (physical responses to threats follow later in this chapter). Resisting is infinitely more difficult, if not impossible, if you are intoxicated or drugged. It is much better to just not put yourself in this situation.

If the party gets too wild, or if you feel threatened or pressured in any way, don't be embarrassed to ask for help or to leave. Do not walk home alone.

Go slow with a new relationship. On your first few dates, tell your friends who he is and where you are going. Let them know what time you expect to get home. Go to a public place with lots of people present. If he makes you feel at all uneasy, call a friend and tell her why. Get someone to pick you up, or take a taxi.

Personal Safety When Walking

1. **AWARENESS:** Avoid walking alone at night, but if you must, stay in well-lit, open areas. Most women want to look their best when going out to a club or a party. They usually dress to attract attention. This is great at the party or the club, but not so great if you walk home alone. Simply stated, you will become a predator magnet. Walk with others.

Stay sober and coherent. Persons under the influence of alcohol or drugs are much more likely to be the victim of a serious crime or accident or to victimize others. This is not the first time you've heard this, nor will it be the last. It is perhaps the most critical component of all personal security plans.

If you are alone, whether you are on or off campus, on a sidewalk, street, or walking across a yard or open area, at an ATM, or heading for a convenience store, you must constantly scan your surroundings. Keep your eyes moving left, right, ahead, and frequently check behind you. Look for movement, and then focus on it to evaluate any potential threat. Look for anyone who is not moving and evaluate.

2. **AVOIDANCE:** What does this mean? Look for dark areas and avoid them. Look for any person or activity that seems out of the ordinary. Whenever possible, walk between the emergency lights scattered along campus. They have a button you can push in case of an emergency that will cause the light to blink and send a location specific alert to campus police.

You should walk with your cell phone in your hand and be prepared to quickly dial 911. If you are talking, you may be able to maintain your awareness, but if you are texting, you cannot. Do not text while walking! Do not walk and have ear buds blocking your hearing! Don't walk into potential high crime areas. The more you have had to drink, the less aware you will be of your surroundings.

71

Keep in mind that many attackers, especially robbers and muggers, begin with brute force and attack without warning. Some do not. Ted Bundy did not. The rapist may begin by trying to coax a woman into a secluded area to then force her to give up her control. In the book, *The Gift of Fear,* the author, Gavin de Becker, calls this behavior "Pre-Incident Indicators." A stranger may try to pretend he has something in common with you. He may be charming (as was Ted Bundy). When people lie, they often embellish details to make themselves seem more believable. Too much information is usually bad information. All the coaxing he does is with the purpose of getting you alone and vulnerable. In his book, de Becker describes a man who persuaded a woman to let him help with her groceries, persuaded her to let him carry them to her door, and persuaded her to let him take them to her kitchen. Each suggestion was met with a "no" from the woman, but he ignored them. She turned over control of the situation to him and was raped and assaulted for hours.

A predator in the wild looks for the weakest and the slowest prey. So will the human predator. His advantage is surprise. He will target a woman who appears to be inattentive, weak, or intoxicated. By keeping your head up, swinging your arms while you walk and appearing alert and confident, he may decide you are not a good target. Don't forget to frequently check behind yourself to make sure you aren't being followed. Listen for footsteps and for cars coming up behind you (whenever possible, it is safer to walk facing oncoming traffic). If a car stops near you, and there is no reason for it, such as a stop light or stop sign, treat it as a potential threat and move away.

Look for anything that is unusual or makes you feel uncomfortable. You can think of that as keeping your "radar" going. Women are considered to have a highly developed "sixth sense," or "women's intuition." Use it. If you see someone or something that doesn't look right, or gives you a funny feeling, your radar, gut instinct, sixth sense, or women's intuition is working. The police call this being "hinky." Trust your intuition. If it feels wrong, it probably is wrong. Do not get close to anyone or anything that gives you this feeling. Immediately head to a well-lit area such as a sorority house, dorm, open store, or even a fraternity house, but be wary of going somewhere that might put you at even greater risk. If you have been followed or otherwise still feel in danger, bang on the door or ring the doorbell. If no one comes immediately, call 911 if you haven't already, and give your location (always pay attention to where you are) and tell them you need help. Say, "I'm being followed. I'm scared." Give the guy's description to the police. They'll be on the way. Tell the potential predator that you have called the police.

Just because a man is headed in your direction doesn't automatically make him a bad guy. That said, if any man you don't know approaches you from any direction and makes you feel "hinky" or sets off your "radar," change course. Make eye contact, but don't smile. You are letting him know that you are alert and can identify him. If he doesn't look at you, pay attention to what he is doing and where he goes. Cross the street to the other side. If he also crosses over, go back to the original side. If he changes again to an intercept course, yell at him, "STAY AWAY FROM ME!" or "LEAVE ME ALONE!" If he doesn't, he has become a threat. Do the same if he suddenly appears.

3. **ESCAPE**: This is what you must do when avoidance hasn't worked. You can get a head start on calling for help if you walk with your cell phone preset to 911, so all you have to do is touch "Send," or have it set to 91 so all you have to do it hit another "1" and "Send." If a situation is developing that doesn't feel right, give the police your location and say, "I need help." Tell them you are being followed and are frightened. If the predator hears this, it may cause him to back off. If he keeps coming toward you, RUN and SCREAM, "I'm being attacked, call 911!"

Many resources recommend shouting "Help" or "Fire" when in trouble. This author suggests those words alone may not provoke the quickest response from anyone hearing them. Those words may be from an era when there were no cell phones, and the police had to be called from a land-line telephone. "Help" alone may cause someone to think, "I'm not going to get involved," or "there's nothing I can do." The word "Fire" alone may cause them to look for the flames or smoke without doing anything, or to assume someone else has called for the fire department. "Help! Call 911!" is a simple and direct message. It goes straight to the brain with no need to ask why someone wants you to call 911. It needs no interpretation. It can be expanded to "Help, I'm being kidnapped (or attacked), call 911."

If the predator begins to get close to you, running with zigzag movements may confuse him or cause him to trip, but it might do the same to you as well. Spike heels will slow you down (walk barefoot or in flats if possible). Be prepared to defend yourself. Do not run into an alley or a dark area. Always run toward the light or a group of people, but evaluate the group before you get too close to them.

Do <u>anything</u> to attract attention. Continue to yell, "Call 911!" If you are carrying a purse, throw it in one direction and run the other. That may be what he was after, and he may stop chasing you. If he doesn't, then it is you he's after. If the predator catches up with you, DO NOT LEAVE WITH HIM! If you do, you will be leaving crime scene number one and going to crime scene number two.

If the bad guy does catch up to you, it is time for the next line of defense.

4. **FIGHT:** This is <u>not</u> where you want to be. Your awareness, avoidance and escape modes have all failed.

If your only alternative is to fight, you should know your legal rights as provided by law. In Florida, you have a right, both morally and legally, to use force in defense of yourself from another's unlawful force. If you are reasonably in fear of imminent great bodily harm or death, you are entitled to defend with deadly force.

Women in states other than Florida should consult their appropriate statutes, but are likely to find similar, if not identical, language. Your state may not have the "stand your ground" provision of Florida Statute 776.012 (no "duty to retreat."). Even in Florida, if you are able to safely retreat, it is usually the better option.

Florida Statutes on Use of Force:
776.012 Use of force in defense of person.

"A person is justified in using force, except deadly force, against another when and to the extent that the person reasonably believes that such conduct is necessary to defend himself or herself or another against the other's imminent use of unlawful force. However, a person is justified in the use of deadly force and does not have a duty to retreat if:

(1) He or she reasonably believes that such force is necessary to prevent imminent death or great bodily harm to himself or herself or another or to prevent the imminent commission of a forcible felony; or

(2) Under those circumstances permitted pursuant to s. 776.013."

776.013 Home protection; use of deadly force; presumption of fear of death or great bodily harm.

"(1) A person is presumed to have held a reasonable fear of imminent peril of death or great bodily harm to himself or herself or another when using defensive force that is intended or likely to cause death or great bodily harm to another if:

(a) The person against whom the defensive force was used was in the process of unlawfully and forcefully entering, or had unlawfully and forcibly entered, a dwelling, residence, or occupied vehicle, or if that person had removed or was attempting to remove another against that person's will from the dwelling, residence, or occupied vehicle; and

(b) The person who uses defensive force knew or had reason to believe that an unlawful and forcible entry or unlawful and forcible act was occurring or had occurred."

During your defense of yourself, if the attacker is injured or killed, you will have to explain your justification for the use of force. As soon as you are in a safe place, call the police. Don't let your attacker tell his side of the story first. He may claim <u>you</u> attacked <u>him</u> without justification. That is one of the reasons you must have made a reasonable effort to extricate yourself from the situation. That is why shouting "Get away from me!" or "Leave me alone!" or just "NO!" is so important. Anyone hearing that can testify that you didn't start the confrontation. If you pepper spray a guy just because you don't like the way his eyes are on you, and you saw no overt action by him to approach you after you tried to move away, you could be in big trouble if he is able to identify you.

A *caveat:* The following information should not be construed as a substitute for a contact self-defense course, which can be taught by the personnel of most police departments, and is usually available on-site to sororities. **The techniques presented here are only an emergency stop-gap to such training. They are an alternative to simply giving up, giving in, and becoming a victim of rape and/or murder.**

Emergency Self-Defense Tactics

This is "Fight" mode. It is your last resort. If you are at this point, you have failed at staying safe. Nevertheless, you must now do everything you can to defend yourself. If you are not carrying an effective self-defense tool such as pepper spray or a stun gun (see Chapter 7), you will have to resort to hand-to-hand combat. This is the absolute least desirable method of self-defense, but if it is your last resort, then fight is what you must do.

Self-defense in "fight" mode does not mean that you are going to stand toe-to-toe with the predator in a fist fight, nor does it mean you are going to try to wrestle him into submission. Unless he is a really small guy and you are a large woman, you'll lose. It is not a Mixed Martial Arts contest where you will go three five-minute rounds to see who can win by knockout, submission, or the judges' ruling. It is a strike fast and strike hard no-rules situation. You have already been selected as prey because the predator thinks you are weak. Do not show that you are going to react—just fight.

You must go from zero to maximum, and do it immediately. Explode into action. Don't take a fighting stance and alert him that you are going to fight back. You must surprise him and hurt him to the point that he will back off or let go of you just long enough for you to RUN and SCREAM. It is all about facilitating your escape in a matter of a few seconds.

This is not a game—it is a matter of survival. You are legally entitled to hurt him, and if you are to get away and survive, that is what you must do. To try all the following defenses would take much longer than you will likely be able to fight. You should know all of these options, and use one or more of them as the opportunity presents itself. Again, it is unlikely that a predator will jump out of the bushes or from a dark area and grab you. Nevertheless, it has happened, and it would be unwise not to anticipate that possibility and to be prepared to deal with it.

If the predator is within arms' length, scratch his **eyes** or forcefully poke a thumb or finger into his eyes. **Gouge** them if you can. Hit him with your spike-heeled shoe. Spike heels are fashionable, but it's really hard to run in them. It's better to walk barefoot carrying one or both in your dominant hand, or in your other hand if you are carrying a self-defense tool in your dominant hand. Spike heels can be an effective self-defense tool.

Make a fist and **jab** him in the throat with your thumb tightly folded against the top of your index finger. Even just pushing hard into his throat will cause pain. Try it yourself. Press your thumb into your throat and your neck and see how little pressure it takes to become very uncomfortable. It is better not to throw a straight-ahead punch. You could break your hand. Instead, deliver a **backhand chop** to his neck with the edge of your hand. You can do the same by making a fist and swinging it backhand so that the bottom of your fist makes contact with his neck or temple.

Use your **elbow** to strike if he is very close to you. It is the hardest part of the body and is effective because it is small and concentrates the force of the blow to a narrow area. The most effective elbow strike is to extend your arm forward or across your chest or abdomen, and then slam it backward or sideways as hard as you can. Clenching your fist seems to help deliver more power. Practice this move. You don't have to hit anyone during practice!

Bite and/or **scratch** any skin that you can find - face, neck, arms and hands. You will leave identifying marks on him, you will have his DNA under your fingernails, and if he has let go of you or backed off, you can RUN and SCREAM. If you have bitten him hard, you will have left your teeth impressions on him. They can be matched with your teeth if he is captured.

If he is closing in on you face first, try to **knee** him forcefully in the groin. He may expect that and block it. You'll get only one shot at that. If you connect, you will temporarily stop him. If you can grab both of his wrists or forearms, and push him backwards, it may help you to score a bulls-eye as he will be limited in bringing his leg up or turning to block your knee. You can also deliver a groin shot by making a **fist** and bringing it up sharply between his legs. Even if just your wrist makes a solid connection, you will hurt him. This is a man's "Achilles Heel." It is the most sensitive and vulnerable-to-pain part of his body. If he doesn't react, you've missed, and there's no point in trying it again. Immediately follow with other strikes, bites and kicks. Don't stop until he lets go.

Do not kick with a forward movement as he may grab your leg and flip you on your back. Use a **side kick** to his knee by pivoting slightly away from him, forcefully extending your leg that is closest to him and slamming the arch or heel of your foot against the inside of his knee. If you are in a position to strike the outside of the knee, that will also be effective. The kneecap is good, but a forceful thrust kick to the side of the knee will do more damage.

If the predator has pulled you all the way into himself face first, use a **head strike**. Lean your head backward, them slam it forward so that the rounded area just above your forehead (one of the hardest points on the human body) strikes his face. The nose is best, but a strike to his eye or mouth or even his chin will also hurt him much more than it will hurt you. If he loosens his grasp on you, RUN and SCREAM.

If he has your back against him, do the **head strike in reverse**. Lean your head forward, then slam the back of it against his face or chin. If he has his arms wrapped around you, and is taller than you, bend your legs and then straighten up fast and hard to hit him under the chin with the top of your head. Use the heel of your hand to make an **upward thrust** to his nose. It will hurt him. Practice this move, too.

Try to **stomp** on his feet. A good connection may break bones. If you are wearing your spike heels, it can produce a lot of pain. It will be difficult for him to try to pursue you after that. Rake your shoe down his shin. It will hurt.

Many commonly carried items can be used in emergency self-defense. Ball point pens can be used as a dagger, a flashlight can be used as an impact device, and hairspray in the eyes will cause temporary visual problems. Nevertheless, there are better self-defense tools you can carry. Those will be discussed in Chapter 7.

A website containing the article "Self Defense Techniques for Kids" suggests that the potential victim shout, "I'm being attacked (or kidnapped). Help!" That is totally appropriate. This source suggests that the child pretend to faint. There are some risks to that alternative. The attacker may simply pick you up if he is larger than you. This could call attention to the situation, but so will continuing to scream.

If the predator has a gun, you are in an extremely bad situation and have a difficult decision to make. One choice is to stay put, be abducted, probably raped, and maybe murdered. The other is to run. Sources claim that even the police, as well-trained as they are, make only 4 of 10 shots, when they are within a range of 3 to 9 feet, due to the stress of the moment. These sources claim that the predator will hit you, a zigzag-running target, only four of one hundred times, and even then, it will most likely not be to a vital organ.

The predator wants you to leave with him. He may decide shooting at you will make too much noise and will likely bring the police. Given what he wants to do with you, you are no good to him dead. He may decide that he doesn't want the police after him for aggravated assault, aggravated battery, or murder.

Nevertheless, getting shot is very bad, and you need to mentally prepare yourself for that eventuality and what you will do.

Remember that Carol DaRonch was the only woman attacked by Ted Bundy who survived unscathed. That was because she fought back.

The bottom line is that you must do anything and everything necessary to escape. Have you ever grabbed and roughly lifted a sleeping cat by the skin on its back? If not, can you at least imagine the cat's reaction? It will yowl (scream), contort, bite, scratch and run away when released. If you are ever attacked, channel your inner feline and <u>do whatever it takes to escape</u>.

Specific self-defense tools will be discussed in Chapter 7.

The information contained in this chapter is not represented as being all-inclusive. It should, however, get you started on the road to awareness of your safety needs and self-protection activities. The options for self-defense as presented are possible actions you can take to avoid becoming a victim. They in no way constitute a complete self-defense course. <u>Take a police-taught self-defense course as soon as possible</u>!

Car Smarts

When approaching your car, look all around it and glance under it for potential predators. Check the front and back seat areas to be sure no one is hiding there. At night, activate the interior lights with your key fob. If your windows are tinted, a flashlight may not provide good illumination of the interior. If your fob will not do this, unlock and open your driver's door to illuminate the interior and then quickly check the front and rear floors as well as the cargo area if it is an SUV.

Get into your car quickly once you have assured it is safe. Have your keys and pepper spray ready. You should have them in your hand before approaching the car. Keys are an adequate makeshift self-defense tool for pressure or punching if you have the largest key sticking out between your fingers and its base against the palm of your hand. Lock your doors immediately after entering. Make sure your windows are rolled up all the way. Don't sit there rummaging through your purse, texting your friend or touching up your makeup. Start your car and leave. With the right tool, a bad guy can break your window and be in your car before you can get it started and drive away.

If you are going to or are at your parked car, and someone comes after you, activate your car alarm with your key fob if able. Test it before you need it. If necessary, play "Ring-Around-the-Rosie" with him. Get to the side or end of the car away from him. When he moves, you move the opposite way, keeping the car between you. SCREAM and yell, "Help! Call 911!"

If the predator tries to force you into a vehicle, make your body go stiff and hang on to the outside of the car, all the while screaming, "Call 911! Help! Call 911!" If you can get your hands on the car keys, throw them as far as you can. Even throwing them into the back seat or just out the window will buy you some time to escape.

In traffic, always leave some space between the front of your car and the one in front of you. This will give you room to maneuver if you need to.

If you are bumped in light or non-existent traffic, particularly by a male driver, with or without male passengers, give a signal to follow you and drive to a gas station or other busy place before getting out of your car. On the way, call 911 and report the incident. Tell them you are on the way to a safe place. Give them your location. If he doesn't follow, try to get his tag number and car description if possible. At the very least, he has committed a hit-and-run. If you are on a busy street, pull over at a safe location. Don't get out of your car until the police arrive. If the guy gets out of his car and walks to yours, crack the window slightly and tell him you have called the police.

Never be sympathetic to a stranger who approaches you at or near your or another's car and asks for assistance. Remember Ted Bundy? This was his technique. Move away. Tell him to go away or leave you alone. Rudeness is better than being a victim. If the stranger is "hinky," activate your car alarm.

Don't hitchhike or pick up a hitchhiker. Even if it is another woman, you won't know whether or not she is "bait" for a carjacking or a criminal herself. Call 911 and report it if she appears to need assistance.

Although Ted Bundy used a Volkswagen "Bug" in his abductions, vans are often involved. Don't park next to a van that is already there. If you are returning to your car, and a van is parked to the left of your car, keep an eye on it and get in the passenger side of your car. Lock the doors immediately. If there is a man in the right-hand seat of the van, or a car, leave and get a police officer, a security officer, or another man you trust to escort you back to your car.

If the predator has somehow gotten into your car, possibly with a gun or a knife, put on your seatbelt and immediately drive forward at about 10 or 15 miles per hour and crash into something—a pole, a support column or even a parked car. The airbags will go off and your seatbelt will restrain you. Unsnap your seatbelt, get out, and run away, screaming! The insurance deductible is a small price to pay for not being raped and/or murdered.

This is a very difficult decision if he has the gun to your head. It might go off. If you have been driving awhile and have to slow down, and if the gun is no longer pointed at you, crash into a <u>fixed</u>

object (not an oncoming car) at 10 or 15 miles per hour. Your alternative is to hope he will be nice to you when he gets you to where he wants to go - and that is very unlikely.

If you are in your attacker's car, or he is driving yours, watch for the right time (not when he is driving at highway speed) and try to scratch his eyes. If he has stopped or is going slowly, you may want to try to get out of the car. Carol DaRonch escaped from Bundy and survived by doing this. If the car is moving, try to tuck and roll. You do not want to hit your head on the pavement or be run over by the rear wheel.

If you are forced into the trunk of the car, try to kick out one of the tail lights and stick your hand through the opening and wave. Anyone should recognize that as a signal of distress and call the police. If you still have your cell phone, call 911 from the trunk. If you are in your car, you can give them a detailed description. If it is his car, try to get enough details before he slams the lid down to be able to report the description to the police.

Keep warm clothes and water in your car in case of a breakdown on an isolated stretch of road. Make sure your doors are locked and activate your emergency flashers. If there is a well-lit and occupied area nearby, go to it, if it appears to be safe. If you are in a desolate area, walk away from your car and hide in some bushes. Carry pepper spray or a stun gun with you. In all these scenarios, you should call 911, let them know where you are, and that you are frightened.

Being Stopped by the Police

If lights looking like those of a police car suddenly come on behind you at night and you can't make a positive identification of it being a law enforcement vehicle, activate your emergency flashers, and pull over into a driveway or at the front of what appears to be an occupied home (cars in the driveway, lights on inside), or into an open convenience store or gas station, or where there are plenty of street lights and traffic. If it is a rotating red or blue light, rather than flashing bar lights that alternate between red and blue, use extra caution. Anyone can purchase such a light, plug it into the car's cigarette lighter, and use it to try to pull over women drivers. If it is a remote area, slow down, activate your emergency flashers and proceed to a safe location. Stick your hand out your window and wave to indicate you intend to pull over up the road. On an Interstate highway, if you are close to an exit, and you can see there are open businesses, it would be a good place to stop.

If you can identify it as a clearly marked police or Highway Patrol car, then pull over when you can do so safely. Check to see that the officer or trooper is wearing a uniform and make sure that he asks for your driver's license. Keep your car doors locked and open your driver's window enough for the officer or trooper to see your face, and to pass your driver's license, registration, and proof of insurance to him or her. The officer or trooper may approach your car on the passenger side. If the law enforcement officer (LEO) asks you to step out of the car you should do so, however, there is generally no reason for an officer to ask anyone, especially a lone female, to exit her car unless there is a suspicion that she is driving under the influence.

If it is an unmarked car at night, call 911 or your local emergency telephone number (in Florida, the Highway Patrol is connected directly by calling *FHP) before stopping, to check if an officer is indeed in the area. When stopping a car, all law enforcement officers are supposed to notify their dispatcher—for their own protection, as well as yours. If you have made that call, and have kept driving, it is unlikely the officer or trooper can successfully charge you with "fleeing and eluding." After stopping, keep your hands where he can see them—preferably on the top of the steering wheel.

These warnings are presented because there have been reports of criminals using the tactic of representing their car as a police vehicle. Blue lights alone may not signify a police vehicle. A rotating red or blue light also may be bogus. Alternating red and blue flashing bar lights are normal on most Law Enforcement vehicles.

ATM Safety

As discussed in earlier sections, a criminal will usually choose to target a woman who appears to be unaware and unprepared. Your attitude and demeanor will play a large part in his decision to attack or not attack.

The location of an ATM is important in your evaluation of its safety. One that is near a corner presents a hiding place for the criminal who wants your money—or you. Choose one that is located near the center of a building and is open to public view. From a police lesson learned the hard way, it's a good idea to round all corners by walking well away from the corner of the building. If the bad guy is hiding and has seen you coming, it's much easier for him to grab you or strike you if you are close to the corner rather than some distance away from it.

Guard your PIN! Do not disclose it to anyone. Do not let anyone get close to you while you are entering it. They might see it, and then grab your card.

Check out the ATM for obstructions to vision of passersby and police by things such as shrubbery, landscaping, signs, and decorative items. Select an ATM in a well-lit location. Try to avoid visiting it at night. Avoid locations that have large perimeter parking lots and many egress points. Those kinds of locations make it easier for the bad guy to get away.

Just as you would do at your residence or anywhere else, scan the environment for people and things that might make you feel "hinky" before you get out of the car. If it doesn't feel right, it probably isn't. If your radar goes off, find another ATM.

Consider using a debit card for your everyday transactions. It's the same as cash, and you can reduce the amount of money you carry and the necessity to visit the ATM.

Are You Being Stalked?

You have a date or two with a guy, and it just doesn't click. You decline further dates. You think it's over, but you begin to notice that wherever you go, he is there, just watching you. You probably are being stalked.

After being in an extended relationship, you break up with him. He begins sending emails, texts or letters, demanding that you get back together. He may send things that make you uncomfortable, like dead flowers or something from around your residence. He phones constantly. He follows you on foot and in your car. One day he threatens because you refuse to get back with him. He is definitely a stalker, and could turn violent.

A person you have never formally met begins professing his love for you by mail, texts, email, or phone and sends you unwanted flowers or gifts. He asks you for a date. One day he approaches you and tries to touch you. You are being stalked.

Someone you have met casually, or never met, shows up, uninvited, at your workplace, dorm, apartment, or sorority. He stands or sits outside for a time, then leaves. One day he may ask for you. He is a stalker.

A "Predatory" stalker may be watching with a sexual attack in mind. You may or may not know him, but you have caught his attention, and he wants you. He may or may not remain in the shadows. He might make obscene phone calls to you. This guy is dangerous. He is thinking rape, and perhaps murder.

Any guy, to whom you have said "NO," who continues to follow or contact you after you have clearly asked him to leave you alone is a stalker.

When you become afraid of the stalker's behavior, the stalking has become a crime. Stalking is defined as:

> "A repetitive pattern of unwanted harassing or threatening behavior committed by one person against another. It is a form of criminal activity composed of a series of actions that individually might be completely legal, such as sending flowers, writing love letters, telephone contact or frequently waiting for someone outside her school or place of work. When these activities are combined with intent to instill fear of injury, they may constitute a criminal pattern of behavior."

Put another way, stalking is a course of conduct, directed at a specific individual that would cause a reasonable person to be afraid. For good reason, stalkers have been called "Psychological Terrorists."

How common is stalking? At some point in their lives, 16 percent of women have been stalked. Men are also stalked, but much less often.

Following the 1989 shooting death of Hollywood actress, Rebecca Schaeffer, in Los Angeles, California, after she opened her door to a man who had been stalking her, all 50 states and D.C. passed anti-stalking laws. They can be found at **The Stalking Resource Center** under **"Criminal Stalking Laws by State."**

Crossing state lines to stalk someone is a federal offense. Use of email and the Internet to stalk someone is called "Cyberstalking." That is also a federal crime.

Stalkers can be very dangerous. Many will make threats. They will do actual violence to their victims 25 to 35 percent of the time. This occurs often with those from prior romantic relationships.

The stalker may use some of the techniques discussed in earlier chapters, as described by author Gavin de Becker, to get close to you and make you like him. Beware of someone who tries to "bond" with you when you have just met. Beware of the guy who does or says anything to try to make you feel that you "owe" him. The guy you just met, who uses charm to make you like him, may or may not be a nice guy. Be careful. Go slow.

When you realize you are being stalked, tell the stalker once and <u>once only</u>, that you wish to have no contact with him and to leave you alone. Do not speak with him again. If he persists, go to the police, preferably with a friend, and give them all the information you have at the time. Download and print a copy of your state's stalking law to take to them. Let them know you will attempt to gather more evidence of the stalking, such as making a diary of the stalking events (who, what, when, where), saving emails, cards, or letters, storing phone messages and texts, and getting statements from friends who have seen the stalking behavior. Consider discretely taking photographs of your stalker in various locations—or having a friend do so. Do not let him see you doing it. Anything that may have been handled by the stalker should be picked up with tweezers and put in a small plastic bag. On the bag, write the date, time, and location it was received by you. When you have compiled this information, take it to the police.

Tell your friends, family, co-workers, dormitory mates, sorority sisters, and the House Mother about the situation. Have a safety plan that includes a reserve set of money, credit cards, medications, important papers, keys, and valuables. Have a safe place to go in the event of an emergency. Change your phone number. Do not answer any calls, texts or other instant messages from someone whose name or number you don't recognize. Have NO contact with the stalker. Tell your friends and family to have NO contact with him.

Above all, you must re-double your "Staying Safe" behavior with respect to your residence, your "out and about" time and with your awareness.

References

Slight Uptick in Crime. (2013, January 14). *FBI*. Retrieved November 16, 2013, from http://www.fbi.gov/news/stories/2013/january/early-2012-crime-statistics/early-2012-crime-statistics

Rogers, A., & Lubin, G. (2013, November 20). The Most Dangerous Colleges In America. *Business Insider*. Retrieved November 16, 2013, from http://www.businessinsider.com/most-dangerous-colleges-in-america-2012-11?op=1

Lopez, A. (2011, August 15). FSU reports high number of alleged on-campus rapes. *Florida Independent*. Retrieved November 16, 2013, from http://www.floridaindependent.com/43627/fsu-rape

Rutgers. (n.d.). Safety & Security. *Home*. Retrieved November 16, 2013, from http://ruoffcampus.rutgers.edu/resources/safety-security/

A Women's Blog on Love, Romances, Marriages, Relationships and Life: 9 Critical Safety Rules for Women. (2012, March 15). *A Women's Blog on Love, Romances, Marriages, Relationships and Life: 9 Critical Safety Rules for Women*. Retrieved November 16, 2013, from http://www.womanatics.com/2012/03/9-critical-safety-rules-for-women.html

Safe, C. (2012, May 9). Top Ten Safety Tips For Female College Students. *CollegeSafecom*. Retrieved November 16, 2013, from http://www.collegesafe.com/index.php/student-safety/top-ten-safety-tips-for-female-college-students

What Every College Girl Needs to Understand. (n.d.). *Date Rape, Campus Safety, Party Safety Tips*. Retrieved November 16, 2013, from http://www.yourbestselfdefenseproducts.com/date_rape_campus_safety

Self Defense for Girls | Things Every College Girl Should Know. (n.d.). *Things Every College Girl Should Know RSS*. Retrieved November 16, 2013, from http://www.everycollegegirl.com/how-to-avoid-dangerous-situations-and-use-basic-self-defense/

SELF DEFENSE PRODUCTS. (n.d.). *Women's Safety and Self Defense Tips*. Retrieved November 16, 2013, from http://www.womenonguard.com/safety_tips.htm#33

Horn, C. V. (2005, April 26). Ten Self Defense Tips for the Average Woman.

Yahoo! Voices. Retrieved November 15, 2013, from
http://www.voices.yahoo.com/ten-self-defense-tips-average-woman-
1064.html?cat+5

Laur, D., & Laur, B. (n.d.). Life. *Power to Change Top 10 Safety Tips For Women
Comments*. Retrieved November 16, 2013, from
http://powertochange.com/life/personalsafetytips/

via, J. (n.d.). Personal Safety Tips for Women. *ABC News*. Retrieved November 16,
2013, from
http://abcnews.go.com/GMA/HealthyWoman/story?id=125859&page=1#.Ubjj6PlO
OSo

Self-Defense. (n.d.). *4collegewomen.org*. Retrieved November 16, 2013, from
http://www.4collegewomen.org/fact-sheets/selfdefense.html

Women's self-defense techniques, female self defense pictures | groin attacks. (n.d.).
Women's self-defense techniques, female self defense pictures | groin attacks.
Retrieved November 16, 2013, from http://www.self-defender.net/article19.htm

Borboa, M. (2013, January 6). Self-defense moves that could save your life. *Health
Wellness RSS*. Retrieved November 16, 2013, from
http://www.sheknows.com/health-and-wellness/articles/979867/self-defense-moves-
that-could-save-your-life

Pinola, M. (2011, July 28). Basic Self-Defense Moves Anyone Can Do (and
Everyone Should Know). *Lifehacker*. Retrieved November 16, 2013, from
http://www.lifehacker.com/5825528/basic-self+defense-moves-anyone-can-do-and-
everyone-should-know

Delaney, M. (n.d.). Self-Defense Tips. *Four Self Defense Tips*. Retrieved November
16, 2013, from http://www.talewins.com/protectyourself/selfdefense.htm

Editor, e. (1999, November 2). How to Grow Godetia (Clarkia Amoena) | eHow.
eHow. Retrieved November 16, 2013, from http://www.ehow.com/list_6699_self-
defense-techniques-kids.html

Collins, R. (n.d.). Self-defense for college students. *Self-defense for college
students*. Retrieved November 16, 2013, from
http://www.ndsu.edu/pubweb/~rcollins/newsletters/defense.html

A Women's Blog on Love, Romances, Marriages, Relationships and Life: 9 Critical
Safety Rules for Women. (2012, March 15). *A Women's Blog on Love, Romances,*

Marriages, Relationships and Life: 9 Critical Safety Rules for Women. Retrieved November 16, 2013, from http://www.womanatics.com/2012/03/9-critical-safety-rules-for-women.html

Woman pulled over by man impersonating police officer. (2013, April 10). *WVEC wvec.com*. Retrieved November 16, 2013, from http://www.wvec.com/my-city/vabeach/Woman-pulled-over-by-person-impersonating-an-officer-202381121.html

Henry, B. (2013, February 21). Authorities hunt for fake police officer who tried to pull wo - WSFA.com: News Weather and Sports for Montgomery, AL.. *Authorities hunt for fake police officer who tried to pull wo - WSFA.com: News Weather and Sports for Montgomery, AL*. Retrieved November 16, 2013, from http://www.wsfa.com/story/21117393/authorities-looking-for-fake-police-officer-who-pulled-over-woman-along-i-65

Crime Prevention: Tip of the Month - November - official website of THE LOS ANGELES POLICE DEPARTMENT. (n.d.). *Crime Prevention: Tip of the Month - November - official website of THE LOS ANGELES POLICE DEPARTMENT*. Retrieved November 16, 2013, from http://www.lapdonline.org/crime_prevention/content_basic_view/7737

7

SELF DEFENSE TOOLS

These tools are for a specific purpose—to hurt or incapacitate an attacker. Used properly, they can help get you out of a bad situation.

The disadvantage of both styles of defense key chains is that they are "up-close and personal" defensive tools. They are better than bare hands, but if you need to use them, you are already in a perilous situation.

CLOSE-QUARTER DEFENSE STICKS are metal shafts about seven inches long, with one blunt end and a more tapered opposite end. It is used in the "hand-to-hand" combat previously described and gives you a slight edge over fighting bare handed.

The stick is held in either an ice pick grip (for hammer fist strikes) or forward grip (for stabbing and pressure point attacks). With keys attached, it can also function as a flailing weapon. As a pressure point and pain compliance device, it can attack any point a finger or thumb can, but with greater penetration because of the smaller surface area at the ends.

With these, there is really no wrong place to strike. The best targets are the groin, ribs, solar plexus, throat, eyes, arm, shin, hip bone, collarbone, ankle and kneecap. To see what it can do, take a ballpoint pen (with the writing tip retracted) and push it against various parts of your body. It won't take a lot of pressure for it to become quite uncomfortable.

CAT DESIGN DEFENSE KEY CHAIN is inexpensive, small and can be effective in close-up self-defense. Its function is as a punching, pressure, or raking device. It, too, is better than your bare hands. The ear shaped points of the tool are sharp and can produce a lot of pain. Look up this tool by using defense key chain in your search engine or by the link provided.

PEPPER SPRAY (OC, Oleoresin Capsicum) is a compound that irritates the eyes and makes them water badly. The active ingredient is also an inflammatory agent that swells up the eyelids and mucous membranes of the upper respiratory tract. It causes pain and, often, temporary blindness. OC is made from the same chemical that makes chili peppers hot, but at higher concentrations.

Studies have shown that pepper spray is very effective even against people who are very intoxicated, on drugs, or suffering a psychotic episode. The effects of pepper spray last from 30-45 minutes, depending on the potency of the spray solution. According to the Journal of Investigative Ophthalmology and Visual Science, eye exposure to OC is not harmful, but repeated exposure can trigger long-term changes in corneal sensitivity.

Pepper Spray is effective up to at least 10 feet, and in some cases up to 20 feet. While most effects are immediate, you should be prepared to move away by side-stepping from the attacker and being prepared to physically defend yourself. After being sprayed, some attackers have been reported as going down like "a ton of bricks," while with others, it took several seconds for the full effects to set in. You should always attempt to keep distance between yourself and the attacker. Aim the spray at his eyes and facial region and release in a 1 to 2 second spray. Move out of the way, keeping your eyes on the threat, and spray repeatedly in 1 to 2 second bursts until the attacker is incapacitated. Once he is stopped, escape immediately, and call the police. As with other self-defense tactics, as soon as the pepper-sprayed person has ceased to be an immediate threat, RUN and SCREAM.

Ballistic stream sprays project a narrow dispersal of OC, which decreases blowback from wind, and which fires up to 10 feet. With all types of OC, if you miss with the first firing, you can "fan" the spray during discharge. Change position after the first stream, and then move your dispersant path from side to side until you have hit the attacker in the face, eyes, nose, and mouth.

Foam dispersant is excellent for blow-back protection and immediate saturation. It sticks to the skin more than the stream spray.

Cone dispersants cover a wider area and may be the best choice in most situations. It is a fine mist that comes out in a forceful spray pattern, usually up to distances of 8-12 feet. The mist is made up of super fine droplets of pepper solution. These droplets help to minimize blow-back of pepper formula on you while it penetrates the attacker's skin pores and mucous membranes. The pattern spreads out to a width of approximately 2 feet at its maximum distance. It covers the whole face and is absorbed into the mucous membranes, causing the eyes to fill with tears, the nose to run, excessive coughing and shortness of breath.

Several pepper spray manufacturers' products contain an ultraviolet dye that will remain long after the effects of the spray have diminished. If a suspect is captured, and the dye remains, it will glow when the police shine a UV light on the suspect. The spray container should be shaken every couple of weeks to assure that there is no settling of the active compounds. It is estimated that it has a shelf life of up to four years. Probably, it would be advisable to replace the pepper spray every couple of years. All states legalize the appropriate use of pepper spray, but several restrict where it may be sold. Florida does not. Before purchasing and preparing to use pepper spray, the laws of your individual state should be researched.

It is recommended that you find a place where you can fire two or three short bursts from your pepper spray canister to get used to its operation. Don't do this where other people could be affected, and make sure the wind is not blowing toward your face. Disclaimer—this is not a product endorsement but rather the presentation of an option: One manufacturer's line of products has a relatively inexpensive twenty-five shot spray that includes a separate practice canister filled with inert contents. That is an effective way to learn to use your spray without irritating yourself or anyone else.

STUN GUNS can be highly effective in an up-close-and-personal encounter. There is a common perception by those who are not familiar with stun guns that they look like a pistol. Law Enforcement personnel carry such a device, but it is a taser, not a stun gun. The taser shoots electrified darts into the person to be subdued. Civilians are prohibited from carrying tasers.

Stun guns are available in various configurations and sizes. Some are small rectangular boxes, a few models of which are about the size of a pack of cigarettes. Flashlight models serve a dual purpose—both as a very bright flashlight, and as a stun gun at the light end of the device.

Stun guns discharge a high voltage current which, when pressed against the attacker, will almost always cause him to be completely incapacitated. Some are sold with a wrist-connected safety pin that will disable the device if it is taken away from the intended victim so as not to be used against her.

The disadvantage of relying on a stun gun is that in order to use it on an attacker, he will have to already be really close to you. If you inadvertently "zap" yourself, you will be the one who collapses. This disadvantage is offset by the fact that before a threat gets close, you can trigger the stun gun and produce a loud crackling sound and a bright flash of electricity between its electrodes. Unless he is highly intoxicated or psychotic, that should stop the predator from coming any closer. Even under those conditions, if pressed against the attacker, the stun gun should completely, but temporarily, incapacitate the threat.

Some stun guns are powered with standard household batteries, and others can be plugged into a household outlet for charging. As they are ineffective when the battery is depleted, it is probably safer to have the plug-in kind. That way, you will always know you have a fully charged stun gun with you when you leave your residence.

As is pepper spray, stun guns are completely legal in Florida. **FS 790.01 Section 4, Carrying Concealed Weapons** provides that "It is not a violation of this section for a person to carry for purposes of lawful self-defense in a concealed manner, (a) a self-defense chemical spray and (b) a non-lethal stun gun or remote stun gun or other non-lethal electric weapon or device which does not fire a dart or a projectile and is designed solely for defensive purposes." Using a stun gun or chemical spray during the commission of any criminal offense is a separate offense and the person can be prosecuted.

Check your own state's laws on pepper spray and stun guns.

KNIVES are generally not a good idea. It is an up-close-and-personal weapon that can be too easily taken away from you and used against you. It is clearly a potentially lethal weapon.

FIREARMS are another option for protection. However, this author strongly discourages the carrying of a firearm at this stage of your life. They are illegal on many campuses. Twenty-two states ban them and twenty-two others leave it up to the individual college or university. A concealed carry permit license is required in all 50 states, however, many have reciprocity with other states. Twenty-four states permit open carrying of handguns with varying degrees of regulation.

Using a firearm creates the possibility of severely injuring or killing the attacker, and even if you are within the law permitting the use of deadly force, that could create an enormous and expensive set of legal issues for you. At the very least, you could be arrested and held in jail pending an investigation. You might shoot an innocent bystander and face manslaughter charges. You could have the gun taken away from you by the predator and be shot by him.

The US Concealed Carry Association, which actively supports the carrying of concealed firearms, obviously recognizes the risks of criminal prosecution and civil liability following a shooting, as it offers insurance coverage of up to $600,000 for bond, criminal and civil legal defense, and for payment of civil judgments.

Stay in the habit of always having your choice of self-defense tool with you. It will do you no good if you have left it at home. Walk with it in your hand and ready to use.

A woman's personal safety is enhanced by awareness and common sense.

Intoxication and inattention deteriorate both.

THE BEST SELF DEFENSE IS TO NEVER NEED IT.

"Be careful out there!"

References

Kubotans. (n.d.). *(Kubatons)*. Retrieved November 21, 2013, from
http://www.misdefenseproducts.com/Kubotans-p-1-c-
628.html?gclid=CKyklpK59LoCFUho7AodjGgAEQ

Horn, C. V. (2005, April 26). Ten Self-Defense Tips for the Average Woman.
Yahoo! Voices. Retrieved November 16, 2013, from
http://www.voices.yahoo.com/ten-self-defense-tips-average-woman-
1064.html?cat+5

Nordqvist, C. (2011, November 25). "What Is Pepper Spray? Is Pepper Spray
Dangerous?" *Medical News Today*. Retrieved from
http://www.medicalnewstoday.com/articles/238262.

Pepper Spray - 100 Top Tips. (n.d.). *Pepper Spray - 100 Top Tips*. Retrieved
November 17, 2013, from http://pepperspray.lifetips.com/faq/0/0/question-
answer/index.html

Self Defense Products. (n.d.). *Pepper Spray*. Retrieved November 17, 2013, from
http://www.apexselfdefense.com/pepper_spray_buyers_guide_s/220.htm

Good, J. (2011, September 11). Pepper Spray With UV Marking Dye. *Self Defense
Tips*. Retrieved November 17, 2013, from http://www.self-defense-jg.com/self-
defense-products/pepper-spray-uv-marking-dye/

ProtectMeFirst.Com. (n.d.). *Stun Gun FAQ*. Retrieved November 17, 2013, from
http://protectmefirst.com/pages/Stun-Gun-FAQ.html

Holm, E. (2007, August 21). Advantages, Disadvantages and Use of Stun Guns.
Articlesbase.com. Retrieved November 17, 2013, from
http://www.articlesbase.com/home-security-articles/advantages-disadvantages-and-
use-of-stun-guns-201822.html

Stun Gun Laws. (n.d.). *Stun Gun Laws*. Retrieved November 17, 2013, from
http://www.stungunlaws.org

Guns on Campus: Overview. (n.d.). *Guns on Campus: Overview*. Retrieved
November 17, 2013, from http://www.ncsl.org/issues-research/educ/guns-on-
campus-overview.aspx

Concealed Carry Permit Reciprocity Maps. (n.d.). *USA Carry*. Retrieved November
16, 2013, from http://www.usacarry.com/concealed_carry_

IBTimes. (2009, August 18). Which states allow open carry in US? (Full List). *International Business Times*. Retrieved November 17, 2013, from http://www.ibtimes.com/which-states-allow-open-carry-us-full-list-312409

Self-Defense Shield. (n.d.). *US Concealed Carry Association*. Retrieved November 17, 2013, from https://www.usconcealedcarry.com/shield/

ABOUT THE AUTHOR

Robert L. Parke is a former St. Petersburg, Florida Police Officer. He served as a Patrol Officer, Field Training Officer, Breathalyzer Operator and Instructor, and Traffic Accident Investigator. He was named Police Officer of the Year in 1965.

He became an insurance investigator and a commercial pilot, holding the Certifications of Flight Instructor and Ground School Instructor for aircraft and instruments.

Mr. Parke earned his licensure as a Private Investigator, and developed a multi-investigator state-wide agency with offices in Tampa and Tallahassee, specializing in workers' compensation, insurance fraud, personal injury and wrongful death investigations. He retired the company to become Chief Investigator of a prominent Tallahassee personal injury law firm.

He earned Certifications as a Legal Investigator and Evidence Photographer, and has written numerous articles for professional journals, contributed a chapter to the text book *Advanced Civil Investigations* (Aviation Accidents) and lectured on various techniques and areas of legal investigation, evidence photography and the ethics of both. He received three Editor-Publisher awards from *The Legal Investigator,* the quarterly publication of the National Association of Legal Investigators, in which he was elected to the offices of Regional Director, Assistant National Director and National Director.

Following his four-year retirement from the law firm in 2008, Mr. Parke joined the staff of Seven Hills Security, a state-wide security agency based in Tallahassee. He is currently assigned to provide security to a Florida State University sorority.

During his careers in Law Enforcement, Civil Investigations and Private Security, he has not seen every possible way people, especially young women, contribute to their own misfortunes, but has seen a great many of them. This book is designed to concisely present researched facts, statistics and the author's personal knowledge from experience and training in such a way that college women in particular, and all young women in general, can understand the risks they face in an unsafe world, and what they can do to avoid those risks.

The story of "Dismal Key" focuses on human trafficking, an issue that impacts around 2.5 million people worldwide.

Sixteen-year-old McKlusky Harvey's parents ship him off to Florida every summer to work on those "behavioral issues" of his. He's actually enjoying himself on his grandfather's fishing boat, until his new girlfriend goes missing. It turns out she was taken by a trio of human traffickers. Other girls are also missing. The traffickers have disappeared into the Ten Thousand Islands and are planning to ship the girls to Cuba for auction. Will McKlusky and ex-CIA agent, Becker get there in time?

Available at www.syppublishing.com and other online bookstores.